MW00744169

BRODSKY AMONG US

BRODSKY AMONG US

A Memoir

ELLENDEA PROFFER TEASLEY

Copyright © 2017 by Ellendea Proffer Teasley

Library of Congress Cataloging-in-Publication Data

Names: Proffer Teasley, Ellendea, 1944- author.

Title: Brodsky among us: a memoir / Ellendea Proffer Teasley.

Description: Boston: Academic Studies Press, 2017. | Series: Jews of Russia & Eastern Europe and their legacy

Identifiers: LCCN 2016052717 (print) | LCCN 2017008511 (ebook)

ISBN 9781618115782 (hardback)
ISBN 9781618115799 (paperback)
ISBN 9781618115805 (e-book)

Subjects: LCSH: Brodsky, Joseph, 1940-1996. | Poets, Russian—20th century—Biography. | BISAC: LITERARY CRITICISM / Russian & Former Soviet Union. | POETRY / Russian & Former Soviet Union.

Classification: LCC PG3479.4.R64 Z846 2017 (print) | LCC PG3479.4.R64 (ebook) | DDC 891.71/44 [B]—dc23

LC record available at https://lccn.loc.gov/2016052717

Book design by Kryon Publishing Services,
www.kryonpublishing.com

Cover design by Jen Stacey.

On the cover: photograph from the book *Portrait of the Poet 1978–1996*, by Marianna Volkova. Reproduced by the author's permission.

Published by Academic Studies Press in 2017
28 Montfern Avenue
Brighton, MA 02135, USA
press@academicstudiespress.com
www.academicstudiespress.com

For Ross

CONTENTS

A WORD ABOUT THE CONTEXT

The world in which Carl Proffer and I met Joseph Brodsky is long gone—really known only to the children of the Cold War—so a few words about the context for this memoir are perhaps necessary for readers unfamiliar with how young Americans experienced that period.

The Cold War began as World War II was ending and military and civilian witnesses saw the Soviet Union's takeover of countries all along its borders. These countries would come to be called the captive or satellite nations, depending on who was speaking. The brutal assimilation of these countries led the United States into a number of wars in response—most notably in Korea and Vietnam—as well as to bloody interference in the politics of Central and South American countries. The Soviet justification for its own unacceptable actions was that their enormous country needed protection—in the form of borderlands—from their enemies; the American justification for its unacceptable actions was that Communism led to tyranny and that it must be stopped wherever it started. This is, of course, a very simplified explanation, but it will do to indicate the atmosphere of mutual suspicion between these two great atomic powers in the 1950s and 1960s.

Russia had a presence in the everyday lives of young Americans in the 1950s and 1960s, and that presence had an emotion attached to it: fear. We hid under our desks during civil defense drills in school, and we knew why our parents were building bomb shelters. Bombs were in our dreams, and the Soviet Union was in our consciousness as a country that crushed revolts in both Hungary and Czechoslovakia. The leaders of the Soviet Union seemed unknowable and that led to a fear that they might attack us first out of paranoia.

As our generation came to adulthood, its other concern was the gradually increasing American involvement in Vietnam, a place where our cousins and brothers would go to fight in what became an incomprehensible war to stop Communism. A draft was in effect, something that makes the young pay attention to the nature of a given war. We paid attention and concluded that this war was not worth the price. Given this looming presence of the Soviet Union, one might presume that Carl and I made the decision to study Russian in the grand tradition of understanding your enemy; but oddly enough, that was not a conscious motivation for either of us: we came to Russian studies out of an interest in one of the world's great literatures. We came to this literature by different paths, but our reaction was the same. This literature—deep, rich, and powerful—was a revelation after French and English literature, which was what we knew. In the nineteenth century Pushkin, Gogol, Tolstoy, Dostoevsky, and Chekhov had somehow emerged from what was mostly an illiterate peasant country. What followed this golden age was Russia's tragic twentieth century, when war, revolution, civil war, and tyranny combined to almost destroy an entire culture. The miracle was that it did not entirely succeed. It was an intense literature, and we were intense people.

Even though Carl Ray Proffer was born in 1938 and I was born in 1944, and we grew up in different parts of the country, we shared one thing: there was nothing about our backgrounds that would have told you that we would have a life dedicated to Russian literature.

Carl Ray Proffer came from parents who had not finished high school, but who had done very well nonetheless. Carl went to the University of Michigan at Ann Arbor intending to be a basketball player or, if that didn't work out, a lawyer. In his first year he had to choose a foreign language to study; he looked at a board listing courses in different languages and saw the Russian alphabet for the first time. He looked at it and said to himself "What an interesting alphabet." He especially noticed the letter "ж," shaped like a butterfly, and it was this beautiful letter that led him to choose Russian, which in turn led him to classes in Russian literature. Carl, who had read so little literature of any kind up to this point, now encountered the writers of the golden age. This very intelligent man, who, with his exceptional memory and superior logic, should have been a lawyer, fell in love with Russian literature. This was a surprise to everyone around him, and his family worried about what kind of career he could have in such an unpromising field. He decided to do his dissertation on Gogol.

In 1962 Carl took his first trip to the Soviet Union and did not have a particularly good time, since the few Russians he was allowed to meet were mostly monitors of foreigners. He did, however, manage to do a lot of traveling around the country and serious research on Gogol. At a young age he became an excellent teacher, translator, and scholar, publishing an enormous amount in a short time. His main subjects—and influences— were Pushkin, Gogol, and Nabokov.

Unlike Carl, I came from a family of readers, although no one was particularly interested in foreign languages. My first Russian contact was with Dostoevsky, whose *Crime and Punishment* I read at the age of thirteen. I was quite aware that I could not really understand the novel, but I felt its force. When I was fifteen, my math teacher, who had learned Russian in the army, lent me a translation of Mayakovsky's poems, and I was impressed, especially by "The Backbone Flute." (I could never have conceived that I would later come to know Lily Brik, the woman who had inspired it.)

I majored in French and Russian and went to graduate school at Indiana University. In my first year of graduate school I read Bulgakov's *The Master and Margarita* and recognized immediately that this novel was going to be my scholarly focus.

I met Carl Proffer for the first time that same year, 1966, at his notorious lecture on *Lolita* (sexual quotes from the novel, shocked émigré ladies, thrilled graduate students). He was a new professor at Indiana and was then working on his second book, *Keys to Lolita*. In the space of two years we fell in love, divorced our partners, and married each other.

In January 1969 we left Indiana on our way to Moscow and a scholarly exchange. We stopped in New York City on the way and had a series of crucial meetings in Manhattan bars. Gleb Struve, a famous émigré literary scholar, met us in the first bar and declared that we should abandon our trip because the Soviets had violently repressed the revolt in Czechoslovakia the previous year: it was immoral, in his view, to even visit the Soviet Union. But nothing could change our minds. We were tired of the polarities of the Cold War, we wanted to see the Soviet Union and decide for ourselves. We were not proud of our own country as it struggled with civil rights for African-Americans and bombed civilians in Cambodia and Vietnam, and this had the effect of making us question Cold War attitudes. We wanted to get to know the Soviet Union better and decide for ourselves.

On our own merits we would certainly not have had entrée into the world of the Soviet intelligentsia. Carl was only thirty-one and quite unknown to scholars in Russia at that time; I was twenty-five and a graduate student writing a dissertation on Bulgakov. We had only one advantage, but it was a remarkable one: we carried with us a letter of introduction from the scholar Clarence Brown to Nadezhda Yakovlevna Mandelstam, the famed memoirist and widow of the great poet Osip Mandelstam. It was thanks to her that we entered the Russian intellectual world. It was she who made the call to Elena Sergeevna Bulgakova, so that I might interview her. This, in turn, led to many other meetings with people of the literary world.

After a few meetings with Nadezhda Yakovlevna alone, we were invited to a soiree in her tiny apartment. She had invited interesting people, among them Lev Kopelev and Raya Orlova, true believers who had become dissidents after Khrushchev's Secret Speech. These generous and energetic people would become our close friends, despite the fact that the first time they came to the Hotel Armenia they unapologetically grabbed all the English-language books we had, saying they needed them more than we did ...

Over the years (we visited roughly once a year until 1980), the Kopelevs—as well as Inna Varlamova, Konstantin Rudnitsky, and many others—arranged for us to see virtually everyone we could have wished to meet in Russia, ranging from the famed literary scholar Mikhail Bakhtin to the working-class dissident Anatoly Marchenko. We received a fast education in current and past Russian literature of the sort no American university could provide at that time, since virtually no works by current writers were even on our reading lists, and at that time very little was available in translation.

These many encounters provided an education in the real history of Russia and the Soviet Union in the form of eyewitness accounts from people of all ages. The majority of ordinary people didn't seem to care; they went on with their daily lives, grateful for the subsidized utilities and the low price of bread. It didn't matter to them that they couldn't travel or watch certain movies or read anything on the forbidden books list. They complained only when they or their children came up against the system, in which there was no legal recourse for those who lacked contacts with the powerful.

The Russians who had accepted us into their lives educated us, instinctively recognizing they could do something with these two young Americans. They took extra time to teach us about their life, about their past, what they expected, and how to look at things from their point of view. I see now that what was fateful was the meeting of a certain kind of culture with a certain kind of temperament. We were young, energetic, and sensitive to the idea of liberation. And, most importantly, we were people for whom thought and action were very close. In the end we acted on our instincts. It was a great privilege to meet the people of the Moscow-Leningrad literary world, but we returned from that six-month stay with strong emotions. Russia was a nation in chains, that was no surprise—but experiencing it was different from reading about it. We were enraged at how intelligent people were forced to live, and I would guess that the seeds of Ardis came from this rage.

After our first few visits to Russia we understood that most Westerners had no idea of the range and richness of the literature now being produced in Soviet Russia, and Carl began to think about a journal that would be devoted to the writers of the Silver Age (the early years of the twentieth century), so often neglected in our Russian studies, and the new ones who deserved translation. He called together a small group of our friends at Indiana University (virtually all of whom went on to become editors of *Russian Literature Triquarterly*) in the fall of 1969 and showed them his proposed table of contents for the first issue of a journal devoted to Russian literature. We were all very excited by the idea, but no one believed it was really possible—who would fund it? Who would buy it? None of us had ever been involved in publishing, and we knew nothing about it. We assumed that this project would develop in the distant future, if at all.

Ardis really began in the spring of 1971. Carl was restless and decided he needed a hobby—printing poetry on a hand press, perhaps. When he called one of the many commercial printers in Ann Arbor (where he was now teaching at the University of Michigan), he was advised to rent something called an IBM composer.

Once he saw what this small machine could do—which included typesetting in Cyrillic—the next step was obvious: we would typeset the journal ourselves and print it in Ann Arbor, where printing was very cheap for runs of less than a thousand copies.

We thought long about the name of this possibly very ephemeral enterprise, and the name that came to us had its source in our Moscow experience of 1969.

In 1969 we were assigned living quarters in the former Hotel Armenia. I will not go into our many strange adventures in this hotel that had never hosted foreigners, I will merely say it was an ideal background for a Nabokov story.

After a few months we became desperate for something new to read in English. At the embassy the newspapers were weeks old, and the library seemed to have stopped with Robert Penn Warren. One day, a few months into this radio silence, a package arrived through the diplomatic pouch. Nabokov had instructed *Playboy* magazine to send Carl advance galleys of *Ada*, so that he could give a comment in the letters column when the magazine ran its excerpt from the new novel. This was mind-bending by itself, but to have the advance galleys of an as yet unpublished Nabokov novel in that charming old-fashioned room in the Hotel Armenia was beyond our wildest fantasies. Although ours was an unusually happy marriage, *Ada* immediately caused a deep rift: we both wanted to read it at the same time. He, of course, was the Nabokov scholar, but I was the more addicted reader, which I felt should count. We began to steal the copy from each other in despicable ways—the phone would ring, Carl would unwisely drop the book to answer it, and I would grab the novel and run to the bathroom to read the next chapter. We gulped the novel down, virtually memorizing certain parts, and forever after *Ada* had a special place in our memories, tied to that hotel, that winter, and our desperate desire to read something new in English to offset the power of the Russian world we were exploring. Something to remind us, perhaps, that we came from the English language—the irony being that the novel was written by a Russian émigré.

That winter we had no idea of how intertwined our lives would become with Russia, how much her suffering and triumph would move us, how our lives would be changed by the people we were meeting, both wonderful and awful. Along with the internally free intelligentsia we also met brutal bureaucrats, charming informers, and the sadly compromised. We had an impulse to help but did not as yet know how. When it came time in 1971 for us to name the publishing house which existed only in our minds, Carl and I thought of *Ada*, which takes place in a mythical place blending features of both Russia and America, and its Ardis, a literary family estate straight out of Jane Austen by way of Tolstoy, transformed by Nabokov's own love for the estates of his Russian childhood.

Carl believed in the absolute value of enlighten-
ment—it had happened to him when he changed
almost overnight from a basketball player who hap-
pened to study Russian into an intellectual who was
committed to serious study. I searched through all the
Russian art books I had for a suitable colophon and
came on a carriage in a Favorsky woodcut. Pushkin had
said that translation was the post horse of enlighten-
ment, and here was the carriage …

In an incredibly short span of time—three months—
we had a thousand copies of *Russian Literature
Triquarterly* delivered to the garage of our small town-
house, paid for by a loan from Carl's father. Once the
journal was through the press, we quickly reprinted
a rare edition of Mandelstam, and the unpublished
1935 version of Bulgakov's play *Zoya's Apartment* in
Russian, which I had been given in Moscow. Years later
the books were better published in every way, but the
charm of the first years was unique. When it came time
to mail out the journal, friends would drop by to help us
put them in envelopes—everyone sitting on the floor
of the living room, eating pizza. It was hard to convey
this reality to our Russian audience, which imagined
something quite different. They assumed we would get
rich publishing Russian literature, so it was difficult
for them to accept the fact that most of the translators
worked for free. In fact, Ardis would not have lasted
a year without the contributions of Slavists and ama-
teurs who worked for the love of the thing. We were a

small press, but we were the largest publishing house devoted to Russian literature outside of Russia, and our impact was much greater than our print runs would indicate. In America our focus was the libraries and the graduate students; in Russia it was the unknown readers who passed our books from hand to hand and even typed up copies to pass on—especially of Nabokov.

I must say a grateful word about the American support—little known to Russians—for our small press. Despite the primitive design and typesetting of our early books, reviewers for the major newspapers and journals quickly saw what we were trying to do and gave us more reviews than we could ever have expected. They knew that financially this was a mad enterprise and did what they could to help. In 1989 I was given a MacArthur grant, which kept us going for a long time. Over time Carl became very good at communicating directly with librarians—one flyer was titled "A Syllogism for Librarians"—and this was vital, because the hardbound library sales paid for the paperback editions. Sometimes we had the feeling that the librarians were making efforts to help Ardis.

When the authorities became aware that we had become publishers, things got more difficult. We were followed, our friends were interrogated by the secret police, and just possessing our books could endanger our readers. We warned everyone who dealt with us that we were of interest to the authorities, which any Russian could have guessed. This atmosphere of coercion and intimidation had the effect of making us defiant. We were afraid for our friends, but oddly not very much for ourselves. I suppose our sense of outrage relativized the fear.

We knew our writers, since we met virtually all the ones that were alive, but we did not know our readers outside of Moscow and Leningrad, and probably never would have met them if it had not been for the Moscow Book Fairs.

The only fair that Carl and I attended together took place in 1977, and it was a remarkable event. It began badly, with the censors trying to take all our books. Luckily I hid the Russian *Lolita* in a cupboard they didn't bother to search. We had to fight to get some of our books back ... Book hunger was a known feature of Russian life, but you didn't really have a measure for it until you saw people standing in line for two hours or more to get into a small booth where they had heard there might be interesting books on display. Readers from all over the Soviet Union made their way to these fairs, and some of them didn't seem like literary readers at all—and these were in a way the most interesting visitors. The intellectuals pushed over to the Nabokov titles and tried to read an entire novel standing, but the working-class/peasant sort of visitors didn't care or know about Nabokov: they went immediately to the biography of Esenin, which featured many photographs, including one never reproduced in the Soviet Union, that of Esenin after his suicide. This biography of the people's poet was in English, but everyone recognized Esenin's face on the cover. Why their reaction was so moving to me, I cannot say. Perhaps they knew who understood them.

Our Russian friendships led to many dramatic events, some of them described in this memoir. Ardis became an essential part of the Soviet literary world as major authors, tired of seeing their works destroyed by censorship, turned to us to publish their books. Ardis became a way station for émigré writers who came out during the 1970s, when controls on emigration were lifted for Jews—and for those who could "prove" they were Jewish.

In 1973 we had moved from the tiny townhouse to an old country club with a vast basement. Now we had room for offices, book storage, and for our many Russian guests, some of whom lived with us for months at a time.

Despite our best efforts to remain literary rather than political, we soon attracted attacks in the Soviet press. We published half in Russian (all of Nabokov and Brodsky, reprints of rare books), half in English (translations and scholarly monographs), roughly four hundred titles in all. The English translations were what made the authorities hesitate to ban us, because we were translating works by Soviet writers (Trifonov, Nagibin, Rasputin, etc.), something they very much valued; thus we were labeled a "complex phenomenon," which meant we were to be watched but not interfered with.

For ten years we had the usual problems of foreigners in the Soviet Union, but it was not until 1979 that we were officially banned, due to the *Metropol'* affair. *Metropol'*, which we published, was a journal put together by a combination of young and established writers, an attempt to make a point about the absurdity of censorship. It was not meant to be political, but its very nature marked it as such in the Soviet context. The leadership was stung by the participation of people like Aksyonov and Voznesenky, stars of Soviet literature. Almost everyone involved was punished, and we were banned from entering Russia. Even after Gorbachev I would have trouble getting into the country and through the airport guards until the early 1990s.

Carl never saw Russia again, since he was diagnosed with cancer in 1982. As he was getting radical chemotherapy at NIH he wrote a book about the women we had met who had conserved the literary documents of Russian culture, *The Widows of Russia*.

Russia was present at his funeral, not only in the form of Russian friends, but also in the form of letters and telegrams from strangers all over the Soviet Union who had heard about Carl from Western radio reports. I remember one telegram that came from the officially atheist Soviet Union while Carl was still conscious, but very sick: "Tell Carl Proffer," it said, "that a mass has been said for him in Leningrad." This made tears come to the agnostic Carl's eyes.

I ran Ardis from 1982 (when Carl was diagnosed and he switched to writing his memoirs, *The Widows of Russia*) until 2002, and during that time it had some of its most important successes in English, such as the *Glasnost* anthology and the annotated translation of *The Master and Margarita*. Bulgakov, whom we also published in Russian, was the clearest example of how a small publishing house in America could influence the Soviet literary process. In the 1980s I began unwillingly to publish Bulgakov's *Collected Works* in Russian, because the Moscow edition appeared to be stalled by the censorship and my scholar friends told me that it was never going to come out and that I should do it. This was an unwise project financially, but I began it. The Ardis books made their way to Russia, and the critic Lakshin wrote a piece in a much-read Moscow newspaper chiding Soviet publishers for not doing Bulgakov: now, he wrote, the collected works are coming out beyond the sea. That was us, working in the Ardis basement in Ann Arbor—beyond the sea and beyond belief.

Ardis was represented at two more book fairs in Moscow, each reflecting the profound changes moving through the political system of the country. In 1987 I still had trouble getting a visa, and Robert Bernstein of Random House had to threaten a boycott by the other American publishers to force the authorities to give me a visa, days into the fair. Again books were confiscated by the censors. When I showed my credentials to the man registering the publishers, he repeated my name in shock and then pulled out a Bulgakov book and asked me to sign it. During this fair Ron Meyer and I were taken to a private room by literary secret policemen and threatened with prosecution for publishing Soviet authors without their permission; I answered that this was not true and that I had signed contracts to prove it. I also said that I preferred dealing with Gorbachev's people rather than Brezhnev's. This made them defensive, and they let me go.

In 1989 everything had changed, but I was still held at passport control, well after my daughter Arabella had already passed through. The passport officer was having long talks on the telephone with the authorities, and I began to be afraid that I would be sent back; but then Ross Teasley appeared, having illegally come through from the waiting room past the guards with Kalashnikovs. He lied convincingly, telling the passport officer that American journalists were waiting outside to interview me. One more call was made to the higher-ups, and I was then allowed to go through. During that fair in 1989 we saw a free public for the first time, and it was exhilarating and incredible.

It was an honor to publish the best Soviet Russian writers, and our work gave all of us who worked at Ardis something precious: we understood the meaning of our life, which was to play a role, however small, in publishing the missing volumes of Russia's lost library. Russian culture gave us many gifts, but none more important than our friendships with some of the most remarkable figures in the Russian intellectual world, including the subject of this memoir. It is hard to convey what is in my heart as I write about all of this: there really is too much to say.

BRODSKY AMONG US

How Do You Like Your Poets?

Poets love to write about poets. A year ago I opened a book by the Russian poet Vladislav Khodasevich at random and read the words, "Alexander Blok was a poet twenty-four hours a day," and I thought of Joseph. I thought of Joseph and then I thought of Borges; this was the first time in my life I had connected these two writers.

When I was eighteen, I was invited to a dinner for Jorge Luis Borges. This was my first intimate literary event and I did not belong there, but being so out of my element was oddly liberating. Borges was treated like a sacred relic by the members of the Spanish department. I remember nothing that he said, only his graciousness. However I do remember something else from that dinner: the man to my right asked me how I liked my poets.

I like certain poems by Yeats, Eliot, and Mayakovsky, I said, trying to conceal vast ignorance.

He said he meant temperament. I did not yet understand the importance of temperament in writers. I was not aware of how some times are for Eliot, some for Yeats, or, as a Russian would say, some times are for Tsvetaeva, some are for Mandelstam.

Now that I have known so many poets, I see that this is a question worth answering. My subject, Joseph Brodsky, who won the Nobel Prize for literature and was the only Russian poet to become

US poet laureate, contended that the lesser could not comment on the greater, but I believe that a cat may look at a king.

Great Bird-Cherry Street, 1969

It is spring in Moscow, but there is very little nature around Nadezhda Mandelstam's little apartment building in a remote section of the city. My husband Carl Proffer and I have been coming to see her since the black ice of February, and she has given us entrée into the literary world. The poet Osip Mandelstam's widow has pale witch eyes, little cat's teeth, and a child's smile with a touch of malice. Nadezhda Yakovlevna is only sixty-nine, but she looks much older and gives a false impression of fragility. She has finished one book of her memoirs, but it is not yet out. We have heard from those who have read the manuscript that it will be a sensation and will polarize the literary world … She asks me: "Will you write about us some day?" I say no. I am twenty-five, and it seems inconceivable that I would ever do such a thing.

On this day we tell her that we are going to Leningrad for a week.

"If you go to Leningrad, I think you would enjoy meeting Brodsky."

She says this and it is exactly as if she already knows what will happen, and maybe she does. She is an expert joiner of fates.

At the time we have no presentiment—Brodsky is just another writer for us to meet. No one else in Moscow has suggested we see him, although many of our friends know him personally.

We have read a few of Brodsky's poems and know the basic facts of his biography: accused of "parasitism" in 1964, he was sentenced to five years of hard labor, then exiled to a village in the Arkhangelsk region. He was released after eighteen months because of a Western press campaign. He is famous for his trial in the West—but only among the relatively small group of literary and politically inclined people who follow such things. *Encounter* magazine reports on him, as do the BBC and Russian newspapers in Paris and New York. This fame is due to a transcript: the journalist Frida Vigdorova sat in the courtroom and took down everything she could, at great risk to herself; however, she was present for only part of the trial, according to Joseph, since she was quickly identified as a journalist. Without her document, published in the main European newspapers, the world would not have read the words of the young poet, so vulnerable yet so dignified, who told the judge that he was no parasite, but rather a poet "who will bring honor and glory to his country."

To Western literary people during the Cold War, this is a shocking thing. To us, however, Brodsky is not a martyr. Context is everything, and our context has radically changed during six months spent in the Soviet literary milieu. Our friend Lev Kopelev, for example, a dissident and a German scholar, served a nine-year sentence in the Gulag; Varlam Shalamov, the only writer to truly make literature out of horror, spent almost twenty-five years in the camps. The writers Sinyavsky and Daniel, tried in 1966, served, respectively, five and six years in the camps for publishing "anti-Soviet propaganda" in the West. Brodsky was lucky, everyone says, that Sartre took an interest in his fate.

Nadezhda has mentioned Brodsky a few times to us, saying that he is a real poet but that he lacks discipline. And, like almost everyone else, she adds that he is a *samouchka*. This means autodidact, but it has nuances; she doesn't mean an autodidact of the David Hume variety. Some of Nadezhda's remarks are mysterious to us: Akhmatova, she says with a sort of special stress, has had a great influence on Brodsky, on how he conducts himself; she says that Brodsky has read Mandelstam's prose and poetry "very closely."

Nadezhda gives us his telephone number and a sealed letter. At this point she has been back in Moscow for only five years after a long period of exile. She lived through Stalin's terror and has long experience with Soviet informers and is therefore very security conscious: the letter is to let Brodsky know we are safe to meet. We do not know what is in the letter, and we do not know whether Nadezhda has sent many Americans to Joseph—I would guess not, given her fear of foreigners at this time.

It does not occur to us for a second to say no to Nadezhda Yakovlevna, to protest that we have too many people to see in Leningrad in a short time. Nadezhda Mandelstam has been one of our earliest guides in this strange Soviet world; she has made the phone calls that opened many doors and archives for us; we agree to see Brodsky simply because she wants us to.

The Muruzi House, 1969

We walk into Joseph Brodsky's tiny room on April 22, 1969, and meet a man who looks like an American graduate student. He is wearing a button-down shirt and corduroys. The very Western corduroys alone are a visual act of rebellion.

The twenty-nine-year-old Brodsky is handsome in a red-haired, freckled, Trintignant style. His personality comes forward to meet you: he engages with humor, intelligence, and a charming smile. He smokes constantly and eloquently.

The most remarkable thing about Joseph Brodsky is his determination to live as if he were free in the eleven time zone prison that is the Soviet Union. In revolt against the culture of "we," he will be nothing if not an individual. His code of behavior is based on his experience under totalitarian rule: a man who does not think for himself, a man who goes along with the group, is part of the evil structure itself.

Joseph is voluble and vulnerable. He brings up his Jewish accent almost immediately; when he was a child, his mother took him to speech therapy to get rid of it, he says, but he refused to go back after one lesson. He is constantly qualifying whatever he has just said, scanning your reactions, seeking areas of agreement. He talks about John Donne and Baratynsky (both poets of thought), then says *da?* to see if you agree. (Later he would use *yah?* this way in English.) This is part of his social courtship pattern. Of course, there is another Joseph, the one who doesn't like you, and that Joseph—whom we rarely see but are often told about—is insolent, arrogant, and boorish. I am reminded of what Mayakovsky's friends said about him—that he had no skin.

Russian poets are treated as almost sacred by their audiences and have an influence comparable to that of a very popular singer-songwriter in the United States. Poets are expected to declaim, to be performers. When Joseph recites his own poetry, he turns into a musical instrument, and the volume and resonance of his voice fill every inch of available air. This voice, coming through his handsome Roman nose, is like the man himself, compelling and memorable.

Joseph reacts to everything in the intellectual environment. He is in the process of generating ideas and images, seeking previously unnoticed connections and telling you about them as they come to him. He brings intense awareness to the conversation, and his charm is partly explained by the way he acts as if your opinions mattered. Judging from his comments about other poets, he appears to be a driven competitor who is sometimes ashamed of his ambition. Philosophically, he takes the position of an almost violent, if unconvincing, stoicism. He talks *we are nothing in the face of death*, but he exudes *I will conquer*.

The poet is quick to say that he is no dissident—he refuses to be defined in any way by opposition to the Soviet government; he prefers to act as if the Soviet regime does not exist. He makes comments to the effect that it is wrong for dissidents to call attention to themselves when the anonymous millions are suffering silently. This makes very little sense to us and indicates a strain of defensiveness. He unwisely attacks people he knows are our friends. His judgments seemed to be based on politics. He could not forgive our friends Lev Kopelev and Raya Orlova for having been Communists, even though now they are dissidents, having left the Party after Khrushchev's speech about Stalin's crimes. Sakharov is their friend, but Joseph feels that nothing excuses a Communist past. (Later I learned that he had gone to Kopelev for advice when he was in Moscow just before his arrest.) I have to tell him several times that these people are our friends before he stops his rant. He is an inveterate advice-giver, and I think he was trying to warn us away from dubious friendships.

From his comments we understand that we are simply the latest foreigners to visit him—before us have come scholars and travelers from Europe and North America. Many of these people will be important to him later in emigration, but for now they are his experience of the free world.

I am aware of Joseph performing as he evaluates us; at the same time I see his intense self-consciousness. He is physically restless, moving around the room picking up things, running his fingers through his hair. His entire body is part of his communication. Even a performance as "the Russian poet" contains a lot of information. Joseph Brodsky is a conquistador by nature, and all the slightly confused smiles and nervous self-deprecation don't conceal that. He is enormously confident about himself as a poet.

As we talk that first day, I watch Joseph getting interested in Carl, who is very tall and looks like Robert Louis Stevenson, according to our Russian friends. Carl has a restrained, skeptical style and is an expert on Gogol, Pushkin, and Nabokov. Nabokov is a current favorite of the intelligentsia, and Carl is actually in correspondence with him, and this is a very interesting thing to Joseph. I have his attention because I am young and female; I am writing my dissertation on Bulgakov, who is of no interest to Joseph, who considers him too popular to be any good. We all enjoy this first wandering conversation in which subjects are picked up and then dropped at high speed.

When we come back a few days later, Joseph is no longer in performance mode. He waves us in although he is in the middle of a phone conversation and, with one eye on us, checking for reactions, is saying *Zdes' sizhu, khui sosu*, which rhymes and means: I'm just sitting here/sucking my dick. We laugh, he laughs, and our friendship with the intimate Joseph Brodsky begins.

We come away from these first contacts energized and exhilarated but also conflicted, because Joseph clearly wants to bend the world to his idea of how it must be. He is consistent only within the boundaries of a poem. His attitudes change with his moods as much as they do with further thought. What is important to him is to *have* the idea, not to test the idea. He brings fierce certainty to whatever concept he favors at a given moment. He is categorical, he pontificates—but his self-deprecating humor and winsome smile undercut all that. Conversation is more than just socializing for him: he is a person who discovers what he thinks as he speaks.

When we are alone, a lot of our discussion is literary: he insists that the uninspiring (in our view) eighteenth-century poet Trediakovsky is remarkable and prefers Baratynsky to Pushkin. We do not agree with these preferences, and all the power of his reasoning cannot sway us. If you are a Russian poet, it is understandable that you wish Pushkin had never existed, just as artists wish Picasso had died early ...

During this visit we come up against the rivalry between Leningrad/Petersburg and Moscow. Leningrad, an artificial city of strict geometry and neo-classical ornament, is the most European city in Russia and considers itself superior to the rest of the country, and Joseph embodies that attitude. Most of the Soviet Union is presumed to be a barbarian wasteland; Moscow is too organically Russian and is the center of power and therefore suspect. We do not agree—we have met highly cultured people in Moscow, and we suspect they exist elsewhere in this vast country.

Joseph speaks as if one is either a cultured person or an ignorant serf. The canon of Western classics cannot really be questioned, since only this knowledge separates one from the ignorant masses. Joseph believes firmly in good taste and bad taste, without really defining these categories, and nothing was more withering than his nasal, emphatic "that's just *mauvais ton*." We question these absolutes, but we understand that in his world this is a way of surviving artistically in an environment of oppressive propaganda meant to destroy the very idea of intellectual elites. Joseph is firmly for individualism, but he does not seem democratic in the least. *Better than* is one of his basic categories, and it is important to him that he is part of an elite.

Joseph is unlike other writers in certain ways: he allows interruption, welcomes it, even. He gives each person who comes to his door a little of his acute attention. He will have hundreds of friends before he is done and thousands of friendly acquaintances. This is atypical for writers, who must work alone in the end. But the categories of introvert and extrovert are useless when applied to Brodsky: he is both at different times. He is sensitive and needs quiet; he also needs people and distraction. He ranges from being afraid of being alone to desperately needing to escape intimacy at a certain moment. Most of the time he is open to the world in an unexpected way.

A few days later, Joseph invites us to a soirée at his place. About thirty of his friends crowd into his tiny quarters and real conversation is almost impossible. I don't understand his reason for doing this—perhaps he has a presentiment that we will matter to him. (We are already feeling that he will matter to us.) Joseph is nervously trying to be a host, checking if everyone has drinks. Carl gently asks him why he is anxious. He says he just wants to do or say "something to fill the emptiness."

We will come to know six or seven of this group well; the rest I will not see for more than thirty years.

Carl is more than equal to what seems like a group interrogation and asks his favorite question in return: do any of you believe in freedom of speech? Everyone says yes at first, and then begins to qualify that answer: freedom, yes, but not for Maoists, not for Marxists, and so on. Carl tells them that they do not believe in freedom of speech then. They think he is naïve to ignore the results of the October Revolution.

Joseph's friends are immensely proud of him and tell us—but never when Joseph can hear—that we are seeing Russia's greatest poet.

We are sorry to say goodbye. We already feel affection for him and worry about his future. During this visit we have registered the three important facts of Joseph Brodsky's existence: he has a bad heart, he is on a trajectory of confrontation with the state, and he is desperate to get out of the Soviet Union. How could we help him?

I would guess that almost every foreign visitor left with this question, and we could only hope that someone would come up with a solution. In 1969 there is really only one possibility Joseph will consider, and that is marriage to a foreigner. Whenever anyone asks if he would go to Israel (fake relatives in Israel were issuing "invitations" by the score to go to that country), he always says no.

We are back in Moscow, getting ready to leave the country when Joseph surprises us with a call: he is in Moscow. We meet him for a very Russian evening of poetry, drinking, and political argument at the home of Andrei Sergeev. Andrei, whom we met at Nadezhda Mandelstam's, is of great significance for Joseph's literary development, since he has done the main translations of Eliot, Frost, and Auden into Russian for the journal *Foreign Literature*. Sergeev is also the person who told Joseph that his poetry shared qualities with W. H. Auden's.

That Joseph has found his way to the English and American poets, first in translation, then in English, is unusual for a Russian poet, it seems to me. I met many who knew Polish, French, and German poetry, but very few who were even interested in Anglo-American verse. Joseph is most influenced by Auden and Frost, who were very un-Russian poets. He likes their restraint, irony, and technical mastery. He has no interest in French poetry—Valéry and Villon never come up. Rilke, obviously an important influence, is never discussed.

At Sergeev's apartment we all take turns reading poems—Carl reads Pushkin in Russian, I read Yeats—and Joseph is unimpressed, saying we lack the dramatic element, which is certainly true. In our culture poetry can be read simply. This evening is our first experience of Joseph's English. He reads an Edward Arlington Robinson poem, and it is utterly incomprehensible. He, however, is convinced that he has done a great job. This is an important piece of information: Joseph reads English with a heavy accent and with entirely Russian intonation—and has no idea that he does so.

The evening then takes an unpleasant turn as Andrei and Joseph attack us for our attitude to the Vietnam War. Like most people our age, we are against the war. Their attitude is that we are fools if we don't destroy Communism everywhere we can. As for the protesting students of America, they say they deserve to be beaten by the police: they are playing politics instead of just being students.

This dispute leads directly into the subject of civil rights. Andrei and Joseph agree that the protesters were complainers, and that any Russian would be glad to live as well as an average black American. Carl is patient even when enraged and just keeps asking questions about how exactly their laws against demonstrations would be applied.

Words, of course, are not actions, even when coming from a poet who sometimes thought they were. Joseph and Andrei are really expressing their rage at the Soviet system in this debate.

At the end of his stay in Moscow, and just before we are to leave, we have a last brief meeting with Joseph in the tiny park in front of the Bolshoi Theater. The three of us sit on a bench as the trees rain down what look like cotton clumps on us. "Akhmatova wrote about these trees," Joseph says. He is a little bereft, a little wistful. It is as if he thinks we might forget him.

He needn't have worried. Joseph Brodsky is a once-in-a-lifetime personality, and it is hard for us to think about him without resorting to the words *destiny* and *fate*, because those words seem to be in the air around him.

Lugano, 1969

We left Russia and spent some time in Oxford that summer before going to meet the Nabokovs in Lugano, where they were hunting butterflies. Later, when Carl told Joseph that his name had come up in the course of our long dinner, the poet was very happy.

Carl and I met both of these remarkable writers in 1969. Only now do I see that these men of different generations and different backgrounds shared a surprising amount: both were from St. Petersburg, a city neither of them would see again after going west; they had careers in both English and Russian; and we published them both in Russian in the 1970s and 1980s. Profoundly anti-Soviet, neither one of them expected that they would have future readers in their native country, and they were surprised and somewhat skeptical when

I told them, in conversations fifteen years apart, that they were highly valued by readers inside the Soviet Union.

I would say that Nabokov wouldn't go back to Russia because he knew it was no longer the country he had known, and that Joseph wouldn't go back because he was sure it was the same country he had left.

Nabokov and Brodsky were both witty people who were sensitive about their literary honor. They were opinionated, ambitious, and intensely competitive They also shared a hostility to what they understood to be Freudian views of the subconscious.

Until the publication of *Lolita*, Nabokov had no financial security. He switched to English to have a career, since the émigré public could not support him and he was certain he would never have a readership in Soviet Russia. He did not imagine that the switch would bring him money—and his first books were quite unsuccessful commercially. Nabokov spoke three languages from childhood—Russian, French, and English; English was actually the first language he learned. He graduated from Cambridge University. There was no question for Nabokov of *writing* in English; the question was *creating* in English, quite a different thing.

Nabokov had a strong physical and psychological presence; one might have guessed he was a writer by his attentiveness, but one could easily imagine that he was an aristocrat or a scientist—both of which happened to be true. He was both educated and cultured to a degree beyond what was possible for Joseph—or

us. He was very funny and free in private conversation—
no topics were off limits with him—but even as he
gossiped about Updike, for example, there was a slight
edge of the *halluciné* deep in other contemplations.
This was quite different from Joseph, who gave the
impression of being completely present and socially
alert at all times.

These two Russian writers were different in terms of
how they approached literature. Nabokov was both an
artist and a scientist; he cared about precision. Joseph
tried to know the world through the ideas he had
already formed about it and often made his feelings
into facts; he didn't much care if he got a detail wrong
if the poetic line was good.

As a result of these conversations in Lugano, the
Nabokovs sent us money to buy presents for Nadezhda
Mandelstam and Joseph Brodsky to take on our next trip.

When we first met him, Joseph was completely
under the spell of Nabokov's prose, but that ended
when he heard how Nabokov reacted to a long poem
we had sent out through diplomatic channels in June
1969. *Gorbunov and Gorchakov*, heavily influenced by
Samuel Beckett (something Russian explications tend
to leave out), seemed to us a masterpiece, transforming
Joseph's time in the psych ward into something soar-
ingly original. It can be seen as a conversation between
two inmates of a madhouse or, alternately (or even
simultaneously), a mind arguing with itself. Technically
it is an unprecedented accomplishment; among other
things, Joseph created a new stanza form for Russian

poetry. It reads as if the writer took in a huge breath and exhaled this long poem in which rhyme and meter themselves become metaphor.

Carl sent a copy to Nabokov after we got back home, hoping he would like it; he did not. Joseph asked Carl what Nabokov thought of it. Carl summarized Nabokov's reaction as tactfully as he could, but Joseph demanded to know everything, and Carl made a decision: in this friendship he would be truthful as much as was possible with Joseph.

Nabokov found the work "flawed by incorrectly accented words, lack of verbal discipline, and an over-abundance of words in general." He softened this criticism somewhat by saying that it would be unfair to discuss aesthetics in view of the ghastly background and suffering reflected in every line.

Nabokov's evaluation was not so different from Nadezhda Mandelstam's—but she saw the power in Joseph's torrent of words. The change in the Russian language was one of the things the older generation was most sensitive to—and in his early work Joseph would freely mix all levels of language, including words that sounded horribly Soviet for the prerevolutionary generation. (Later Joseph himself—attitudes harden-ing along with arteries, as is so often the case—would inveigh against the use of "street" language in American poetry.)

Joseph never forgot or forgave this criticism. In one moment, he demoted Nabokov from the status of a brilliant writer of prose to that of a failed poet.

For all they have in common, these two writers are not really comparable: Nabokov's prose is vastly better than Brodsky's, and Brodsky's poetry is vastly better than Nabokov's.

New Year's Eve, 1970

Over the next few years we saw Joseph every time we went to Russia, and we got to know him much better. What I remember about Joseph's style in Russian— and I still hear him in my head—was his drawling *tak*, meaning "so" but carrying the idea of "tell me more." Many comments would begin: *vse ochen' prosto* (it's really very simple). He was a master of casual profanity and taught me all the words I was not supposed to know. He favored the words *therefore, consequently, conclusively* … There was a strong attraction to the language of logical argument, no matter how emotional the content. (Later, in English, he would end statements with: *it's as simple as that*, though it rarely was; soon after came the era of the royal *we* and the much-used *at the very least* …)

He was even more funny and engaging as he relaxed into friendship. One of my favorite moments happened when we were in his room and Carl was talking to someone else. Joseph asked me if I knew the famous song from the 1920s "Kupite bubliki" (Buy my rolls). I said I did not. Listen, he said, you'll like the words. And there, perched on the edge of the little leather settee, utterly uninhibited, he sang it for me. It was a great, comic performance of a street vendor's lament: "My sister walks the streets/she doesn't sleep at night/My little brother is a pickpocket."

We had read a lot of his poems by the next time we saw him, a year later. Some people believed him when he said he had no fear of death, but we did not. This was the attitude he thought one should take, but it was not what he lived. What he lived was the fear that he might die at any moment from a heart attack; he was almost terrorized by this when he was alone for too long or with people he didn't have a sense of intimacy with, which amounted to the same thing. His poetry reveals a persistent imagining of a world without the poet, a kind of future-oriented elegy.

Joseph Brodsky was present in our life even when we were back in America. He sent us funny little notes with returning travelers when he could, and we sent him letters; there were also rare phone calls. At this time, for reasons known only to the god of compulsive readers, I was deep in Byron's letters, and Joseph's notes to us were amazingly similar: laconic, funny, and direct. The two poets share many qualities—mood swings, an inclination to fall in love easily, and the ability to inspire deep loyalty in their friends ...

In answer to one of Joseph's postcards of distress, Carl wrote him, for example: "To be serious a moment, George [Kline], E. and I spoke long and lovingly of you. He showed us his pictures of you, one with north-ern forest as background, which made E. cry, me angry ... In your letter you mention more recent depression. You must kill *Malone Dies*. I have no certain suggestions what weapon to use, but you must, one must in general. If you can send part of the depression away in letters, then send them to us. We can bear it, because we have more than our share of joy."

Depression was a danger for this poet. This is a from a letter written in English, dated June 24, 1971, which began "Dear dear Carlendear": "Finishing this letter I feel again some kind of depression ... In any case I want to say you for you will remember always, because I see that I shall use this word less and less, that I really love you, with all my heart, with all my soul and with everything which remained in my mind ... Because on your faces is written more than one could write on the paper. Forgive me."

Russian readers often accused Joseph of coldness, but I never saw that in his poems; rather, I saw someone refusing to give in to his own fear by saying preemptively: we are nothing in the grand scheme of things. His attitude reflects that of the dark realist, but the poetry has an ebullience that cuts against this attitude. Joseph's technical virtuosity, his delight in, say, forming the shape of the butterfly with his lines in "The Butterfly" induces joy because the poet himself is joyful as he composes it. Joseph's innate interests were metaphysical, and yet I could almost make a case that he is a romantic: his greatest poetic project turned out to be a large number of interrelated poems about his love for one woman.

Joseph had an enormous number of Russian acquaintances, and he had come to know the literary elite, the young poets around Akhmatova, the linguists of the Tartu school (the Soviet successor to the Prague Circle). He had left school at fifteen, which meant that he had to take numerous odd jobs, but he was free to read what he found interesting. Later on he made his way to the most highly qualified sources of literary education by auditing courses and meeting academics. My sense was that he really could not be taught, so school (especially Soviet school) was probably unbearable to him; he was, however, excellent at learning on his own—but only about subjects that interested him. Joseph's poetic personality had formed early: he sought what fit into his worldview from almost the beginning. He did not have to read all of a book to get his particular response to it, and he was the same when he listened to intelligent conversations—he would snatch the ideas he needed out of the air.

This early academic departure resulted in some fairly large gaps in his knowledge, and he didn't know what he didn't know. Essentially, Joseph was the only expert in his mental world. He justified the decision to leave school in different ways, most consistently as an ethical decision: he saw that those who went through Soviet education lost their independence. However we all knew many physicists, linguists, and artists, for example, who went through the system and were perfectly able to think for themselves. Once he told me he left because of a girl, and that did seem like him.

I am always surprised at the knowledge ascribed to creative writers by critics, as if writers are supposed to be scholar-philosophers. Some are—Frost was a leading Latinist of his generation, and Eliot knew at least four languages, two of them dead—but most are not. It is not erudition that makes the poet.

Joseph's grand generalizations didn't always withstand analysis—the one, for example, which claimed that falling empires were held together by language alone. Just as artists privilege the image, Joseph's deification of language itself is part of his *déformation professionelle*. He thought if leaders read more poetry, it could save the world from tyranny as leaders learned to respect language itself. This large claim reflects his ambition: it was not enough for him that poetry be art, pleasure, and consolation; he wanted it to lead to something much bigger.

He is on record as saying that prose has no rules, a stance that enraged the prose writers who read his comments about the superiority of poetry to prose. And yet he often talked about wanting poetry to have a prose quality, something like Dostoevsky. Never, never did he invoke in my presence the most acclaimed novel in verse, *Eugene Onegin*.

He did not always read long prose works to the end. Poetry, of course, he read thoroughly, even bad poetry, and he memorized great amounts of it. "You never know who might have a good line," he would say.

Anna Akhmatova often came up in his conversation; he spoke as if he fully understood her significance only after her death. She was Joseph's first famous mentor. When he met her, in 1962, she was the only widely acclaimed Russian poet alive—Pasternak had died in 1960. Several of Joseph's friends had known Pasternak well; there was a difference between these two famous poets: Akhmatova was generous with the young, whereas Pasternak was not. When Akhmatova went to Oxford to receive an award, she told her friends and acquaintances there all about the young Joseph Brodsky; so when he later left his country, the path had already been prepared for him. Akhmatova can truly be said to have influenced Joseph's fate.

Joseph was frank in telling us that he didn't really like her poetry; Akhmatova, uncomfortably penetrating where opinions of her poetry were concerned, saw that his poetry was very different from hers, which was deceptively simple. He told me she said to him that she didn't believe that he could possibly like her poetry. He, of course, gallantly denied that. My opinion is that she saw through this, just as Akhmadulina would later.

Once, when I was having writer's block, he said that Akhmatova had a prescription for that: one must immediately start another large project, and that would loosen things up ... It was odd and wonderful to hear Akhmatova's words through him—unlike Joseph, I did like her poetry and found her personality and her life fascinating.

Joseph was affected by Akhmatova's ability to forgive the people who had killed her husbands and imprisoned her son. What he knew about applied Christianity came through her. She had in a sense prepared him for his trial by demonstrating how one should conduct oneself as a poet, but even more importantly, he recognized in her that rare person who had something to teach him about how to be an evolved human being.

During our various visits to Leningrad Joseph invited only a small group of his friends to see us, and half of them were not Russian. They included Leonid Chertkov and his wife Tanya Nikolskaya, both literary scholars; Tomas Venclova, the Lithuanian poet; and Romas (Ramunas) Katilius, a Lithuanian physicist and his Uzbek wife, Elia, also a scientist.

Joseph in real conversation differed from the later Joseph of formal interviews, whether filmed or written. In the interviews he is performing, calculating effects, indulging in monologues, and the other side of the conversation is of little importance to him. In real life, conversations had many sides and Joseph's friends, including us, did not always agree with him or let things slide out of respect for his talent. We behaved like equals.

In this period Joseph could accept criticism from certain people, especially Chertkov, a poet and literary scholar seven years older than he who had served five years in the camps for taking part in a protest against the Soviet invasion of Hungary. When Chertkov spoke, Joseph listened. The same was true of Tomas Venclova and Romas Katilius, although they were less direct than Chertkov was.

These were the people present for our visit in 1970 over New Year's Eve, when it was brought home to us just how dangerous Joseph's personality was for his situation. We were going to share the New Year's celebration with Joseph and a few of his close friends. This day we were in his room with Romas, who was looking for something in the drawer of Joseph's table. Carl wrote everything down in code the next day:

> He [Romas, called "Robert" in the notes to protect his identity] saw a small MS, and he took it out. He read it, looked stunned, then gave it to Ellendea, who read it and was also obviously horrified, and finally I read it. Romas took it back, made a correction in it, and Joseph said sharply, "Ne ty napisal, a ia" (You didn't write it, I did). "I know that kind of stuff," he said, adding that it was a rough draft, that it would not be finished for two days yet.
>
> The letter was addressed to Brezhnev. It dealt with the death sentences handed down after the "trial of the 14" (who planned to hijack a plane) to Eduard Kuznetsov and his cohort Dymshits.
>
> The letter began, roughly, "As a citizen, as a writer, as a human being ..." It was a plea for the death sentences to be commuted.
>
> "Blood is poor building material," Joseph wrote. He used comparisons of the present Soviet government with other regimes, including the Nazis and the Tsarists. He drew parallels between the Germans and the Soviets in their anti-Semitic attitudes. He saw it as official policy, and compared it, in this, to the regime of the Tsars, when the Pale

had been invented. He wrote that the people have had enough suffering already, so why should there be the addition of capital punishment.

Obviously, the sending of such a letter could have had very serious effects on Joseph's future freedom. Exactly what they might be was a subject of intense debate a couple of nights later.

For the moment, Romas engaged Joseph in a debate about purely legalistic matters. He said that Joseph had made a mistake in saying that there was nothing in the Criminal Code about receiving the death penalty for the mere intent to commit a crime, and in writing that in no place in the world is intent equal to commission.

Joseph challenged him, and got down a copy of the Code itself. Romas read for a few minutes, then found the section that proved that intent is tantamount to act. Joseph surrendered the point. Romas said it was that way in all countries that inherited the Napoleonic Code (in whatever form). Joseph said that ordinarily he did not read the Code (since from the regime's point of view it is an empty formality anyway), but that he had specifically got a copy to check this point. It was typical of him to find the wrong conclusion in the source he sought, so strong were his own opinions about how things ought to be.

Both of them, incidentally, agreed that the trial had occurred only thanks to a provocateur, since the papers normally never printed anything until after at least a month of checking, but that in this case the papers reported it all the next day. They speculated that one of the two getting the death sentence was probably the provocateur. I report this as typical Soviet psychology, not as a fact about the defendants.

—Carl Proffer, *Joseph Brodsky: Notes for a Memoir*, 1984

What I still remember about this letter is the cold fear that ran through my body as I read it: Joseph really intended to send it, and he would be arrested for it. It also occurred to me that Joseph had an unrealistic idea of how much the people at the very top cared about poets who were as yet unpublished in the Soviet Union—he was not Solzhenitsyn. He had, however, taken part in a Moscow poetry event with the stars of the Soviet literary scene—Evtushenko, Voznesensky, and Akhmadulina. These were poets who sold out stadiums. Joseph had been published abroad, mostly in places the KGB would not bother to monitor, and these poems were not openly political. I would guess he simply thought it was part of a poet's duty to react to injustice, that his gift itself justified such reactions. I had learned few Russian proverbs, but I knew the one that Carl and Romas were thinking of: "If you've tasted prison food once, you'll taste it again."

It did not help that Joseph himself had been implicated years before in an aborted attempt to hijack a plane. This was not a false story.

Much to everyone's relief, news came within a day or so that the death sentences were commuted to hard labor. Our concern about Joseph's future intensified after this: he had to be gotten out before he did something even more provocative.

We brought our three young sons with us on this New Year's trip. Joseph happily carried our youngest son on his shoulders through his building's corridor—Ian, close to his own son in age, would always be his favorite.

Meeting our children inspired Joseph to try to arrange for us to meet his ex-wife and son. (The couple had not been officially married, so no divorce was involved, but Joseph considered her his wife.) Her child was given her last name, supposedly so that he would not be marked as a Jew. This was Joseph's last chance to introduce us, since we were about to go back to Moscow and then home. He addressed Marina as "Basmanova" on the phone and asked her to bring his son, Andrei, to meet our family at a nearby park. Marina, of course, arrived without Andrei. She was a tall, attractive brunette, inclined to silence, but beautiful when she laughed—and she laughed because as she came up to us Joseph was teaching me how to pronounce correctly the word *svoloch'* (bastard).

My first impression was that she was an interesting, if difficult, person. She was with us a very short time. We soon understood this was a very important meeting: we had just met the woman who made him as a poet.

Joseph was our host for this memorable New Year's with Tomas Venclova, Andrei Sergeev, and the Chertkovs. Joseph's mother, Maria Moiseevna, had cooked wonderful food and had put out her best silver and china; she did not stay with us, which was just as well, for the drinking got very serious.

Later when I read Joseph's moving essay on his parents and got to the part where he states that his parents had little self-awareness, I wanted to throw the book across the room. In his essay Joseph mixes categories: his parents were unlike him in that although they were educated, they were not intellectuals—it really did not have to do with the generational divide.

These parents had been born into a briefly free world and then shaped by life under Stalin, a life in which your deepest thoughts were best unshared—especially with your hell-bent, risk-taking son who appeared to have no concern about how his actions would affect his parents. It was the policy of the Soviet Union to punish the family as well as the offender, and we all knew why his parents were not allowed out to visit him: punishment was still in effect, and Joseph had quarreled with the influential people who might have gotten this travel ban lifted.

Maria Brodsky was a warm, intelligent presence. Joseph had been very spoiled by her—his father was away at war within a year of his birth and did not return until Joseph was eight. She was from Latvia, was bilingual in German and Russian, and had worked at various places (including a prisoner of war camp and the Leningrad prison) as a bookkeeper and an interpreter.

Joseph's father, Alexander, was a different, colder, story, at least in my experience. He had studied geography and during the war he became a military photographer. When he returned to the family with the rank of captain in the Soviet navy, he was determined to discipline the young Joseph, but nothing worked: this child would not be changed, even by beatings.

Although living in a room that was actually a corner of his parents' larger room was difficult, it was useful in another way: Joseph paid no rent, and his mother was always ready to feed him. Unlike his peers, who had regular jobs, Joseph could stay home and translate for a minimal living.

This New Year's Eve Joseph was happily high, and his subjects were death, Samuel Beckett, and the beautiful American woman who was with us on the trip. This woman, sensing Joseph's intention, had stayed back at the hotel, but he was determined to be with her. After some late-night phone calls to her, he accompanied us back to the hotel and persuaded her to spend the rest of the night with him. This was our first experience of Joseph's romantic will, and it was impressive.

The next day, New Year's Day, 1971, we went to Romas and Elia's, where Chertkov and Joseph had a nasty fight about the letter to Brezhnev and the idea of justice. Chertkov ridiculed Joseph for his boyish belief that the letter represented a significant moral act. This degenerated into Joseph actually saying that it would be better to be dead than red and that ideas are supreme in art. No, said Chertkov, ideas kill art.

What about "thou shalt not kill"? asked Joseph.

That idea killed more people than any other idea, Chertkov answered, and then, in the face of Joseph's incomprehension, had to explain he meant the Inquisition and the Crusades.

This was a cutting free-for-all, and it wound back to Joseph's saying that Vietnam should be turned into a parking lot and that the black power movement should be put down. Chertkov called him out for racism, and Joseph said he was joking. (I think he was aware at this moment that he was surrounded by people who believed in tolerance. If Sergeev had been there, he would not have backed down.)

Chertkov was not inclined to let him off. They had clearly had this fight before. No, this comes up too frequently and insistently with you to be a joke, Chertkov snarled. Tomas Venclova, who had a much calmer temperament, had to intervene by pretending to explain to us in a loud voice that these were just student-style arguments.

Sadly, they weren't. This friendship was changing in front of us in the course of these quarrels. Joseph could be immensely categorical, and he had little tolerance for tolerance where Soviet power was concerned. He was intemperate, to put it mildly; it is a miracle that our friendship did not break early on the rocks of political disagreements.

Later, in the hall as we were leaving, having felt that he had not been seen in the best light, Joseph told Carl: "Nevertheless, justice is more important than art, than all the Pushkins and Nabokovs. New Pushkins and Nabokovs will always be born anyway—but justice will not always be found."

This, in a sense, is always true, but Joseph did not consider the question of what justice might mean to different people. He was no monument to justice, but then neither were we: we were all people of strong attachments and passions, and we understood this about each other.

The Roof of the Peter and Paul Fortress

It is May 10, 1972, and we are in Joseph's room. The Soviet government has started the big cleanup in anticipation of President Nixon's arrival to put the finishing touches on détente, a cleanup that includes laying new asphalt as well as disposing of dissidents.

Joseph is discussing yet another possible fictitious marriage. (Marrying a foreign woman has come up a lot with him. Earlier he had proposed to Faith Wigzell, an English Slavist, but that would have been a real marriage.) We are against one of this year's candidates—she seems unstable and quite likely to refuse to divorce him once he is in America ... In the middle of this conversation the telephone rings. (Joseph always answers the phone, no matter what is happening.) He says little, and when he hangs up he looks confounded.

"Such things don't happen," he said, doing the lightning analysis of a Soviet citizen in contact with the state.

He explains: he has just gotten an invitation from OVIR [the Office of Visas and Registration, involved in the granting of exit visas, among other things], asking if he has the time to drop by that afternoon.

Nixon's visit was the key factor, I think, in this unusual development. It has been a time of change: the previous October Sakharov had called for free emigration, and the dissident Bukovsky was put on trial that January.

We have come to visit Joseph, a fact the authorities are well aware of, since they were following us everywhere in Moscow, and are now doing so in Leningrad. Perhaps they think we might help them in their project—and in a sense they are right.

Our status in Russia has changed—we are more at risk, more interesting to the authorities. In 1971 we began Ardis, and published Joseph's poems in the first issue of *Russian Literature Triquarterly* in both Russian and English, and included many photographs of him as well. This was Joseph's first extensive publication in the United States. In Moscow we have been warned by friends who have friends in high, dark places that the KGB is aware of all these activities.

In this year the idea of emigration is being discussed at almost every kitchen table in Russia. It is remarkable how similarly very different people talk about why they want to go: I know what my future is here, there are no surprises; I want something different, even if it's hard.

I heard this many times, including from Joseph. No
one believed us when we said that it would be difficult
for them in our country because they were sure their
education and intelligence would overcome all prob-
lems.

Joseph walked us to the bus stop, overwhelmed by
supposition; we agreed to meet later that day after the
interview. When we saw him again, he was a combi-
nation of excited and disoriented. The OVIR officer
said that Joseph should go now, because "a hot time
was coming." (These were the exact words, and we all
parsed them: a hot time, as in summer, a hot time, as
in arrest and imprisonment.) If Brodsky agrees to emi-
grate to Israel, the officer promises, he can go within
ten days.

Here was the special offer, at a moment when Joseph
is desperate to get out, and he was going to accept it.
The alternative was going to be something involving
prison, he was certain of that, and he would not take
that risk.

Later that day we met again and brought our chil-
dren with us. Carl, aware that history was being made,
wrote down in code what happened next as soon as we
got back to our hotel:

> What was he going to do now, Joseph asked us, as
> we sat facing each other in his room (the pictures
> of us, him and the children are from this day). "It's
> easy," I said, you'll become poet-in-residence at
> the University of Michigan."

I had no idea if this were something I could pull off at all, but I thought it was essential to act positive. Even Ellendea looked askance; she knew what he didn't know, that even within our department there were probably only two or three people who had ever read a poem by Brodsky, and what their attitude would be towards making him a colleague was a real mystery. In any case Joseph was still worried about the actual future, and since he was afraid the room was bugged, he suggested we go for a walk.

And so we went, Joseph, Ellendea, Andrew, Christopher, Ian and I, on a long and tiring tour from Joseph's apartment, across the Neva, to the Peter-Paul Fortress, celebrated as the prison for Russian writers (Dostoevsky, Chernyshevsky, Ryleev, Kyukhelbeker and Gorky, to name only a few). While it wasn't the first Frisbee Leningrad had seen, it was pretty unusual to see all of us playing with it across town and inside the courtyard of the fortress, just down the way from the gloriously handsome church where most of the Tsars of Russia, from Peter the Great to Alexander III, are buried. We attracted a lot of attention, and Joseph used the quickly changing positions created by the escaping Frisbee to check for tails. Finally he guided us through the innards of the prison and up onto the roof of the fortress. We all clambered across the ramparts and tacky roof, to a corner battlement where Joseph said he had spent a lot of time. From there one could look down on the sunbathers lined up against the fortress wall by the Neva, and one could make sure that no one was close enough to listen.

In this odd location we discussed all the problems we might face in the next few weeks. We talked about what I would do when I got back to Ann Arbor, how we would manage to discuss the results over the phone (we picked code words for the key concepts).

Ellendea and I promised that from the time he got to Vienna he would be cared for, indeed, it was likely that I would fly to Vienna myself to meet him when he arrived. With luck the university would send me officially, but if not I would be there anyway. The formalities would probably be extensive (again, we had no idea how extensive, corrupt, and enraging the American red tape would be). We speculated about his future; then, as later, I said the first year or two would not be the problem; it would be the period after which any Russian celebrity had to fear, the period after the honeymoon of scandal, dissent and novelty.

—Carl Proffer, *Joseph Brodsky: Notes for a Memoir, 1984*

Joseph was not interested in going to Israel, nor did he want to go to live in England or France: he wanted to go to the anti-Soviet great power. It is important to underscore the fact that he knew where he was going from the day of the OVIR interview, because later accounts (such as his own *Paris Review* interview), would contradict this, as he portrayed himself as completely unsure of where to go for reasons I cannot imagine. Joseph was prey to many kinds of guilt, and perhaps that came into play here, but the fact was he had only one place in mind.

Later, much later, Joseph would say he had been thrown out, exiled, that he had gone against his will— but that was in another world, another key. We were there at the moment, and we felt overwhelming relief. Yes, he was leaving family and friends and that would be very hard; but Joseph would write poetry, he would get decent medical care—he would live.

The news spread quickly through his Leningrad circles. Before we left the city one of his friends, worried about what we were taking on if he came to us, said: "He fights with everyone sooner or later, and he will fight with you."

But it was too late for warnings.

The Schwarzenberg Palace: 1972

Joseph lived in the moment and was sometimes overly optimistic. That he was leaving his country was clear to him, but he did not seem really to believe that he might never see his friends and family again. Somehow he was sure that they would all come to visit.

Joseph was by all accounts nervous and excited to leave; his friends and family saw him off. He knew that Carl was coming to meet him in Vienna.

Joseph had already informed his net of foreign contacts that he was coming, and many projects were already in the works. One crucial person was George Kline, Joseph's translator and a professor at Bryn Mawr. He was working on what would become the Penguin edition of Brodsky's *Selected Poems* (1973), Joseph's first major book in English. George had published many of the poems in various periodicals and was doing his best to make sure Joseph's presence was anticipated.

Carl's task was enormous. He had to get the university to hire a Russian poet—sight unseen, poems unread—and make him writer-in-residence. This required persuasion directed at department heads and deans. The deans were not people who kept up on literary events in the Soviet Union, and they had no idea who Joseph Brodsky was. Luckily, Carl knew how to make a case—he assembled relevant materials, he convinced them that the addition of Joseph Brodsky to the faculty would someday be to their credit. He emphasized the drama of a poet being exiled from his country for being a nonconformist. He also let them think Joseph's English was fluent. Carl was the youngest full professor in Michigan's history, and the university's powers were inclined to trust him. As an ex-basketball player he knew to move fast when he saw an opening.

Joseph was very happy later, when he found out that Robert Frost and W. H. Auden had preceded him in the post at this university, but at the time we did not know this.

In the end Carl got what he wanted. Now there would be the colossal battle with bureaucracy, a battle Joseph had little understanding of: how do you get someone into the United States when his visa is for Israel?

Carl flew to meet Joseph in Vienna, just as he had promised, and we kept in touch by phone. These were the days of expensive long distance—no Internet, no cell phones. Carl paid for his ticket to Vienna and for the hotel he and Joseph stayed in, as well as for the car they would rent. Ardis had begun, but there was really no money for all this—without credit cards it would have been impossible. Carl had made his decision long before that Joseph was worth a great deal of trouble.

Carl got there early:

> It was Sunday, June 4, and the flight arrived more or less on time at 5:35. As the bus approached from the plane I saw Joseph in the window, and he saw me. He gave a V-for-victory finger flash. Downstairs at the window there was a ten-minute delay when one of his two bags was lost, the first of a series of mechanical details that would slow everything down for days. As Joseph emerged and we embraced, I discovered that a Viennese with strong ties to Russia, Elizabeth Markstein, and her husband were also there to meet him. He and I took a cab together; his repeated reactions were ones of nervousness, saying "strange, no feelings, nothing," a bit like Gogol's madman. The number of signs made

his head spin, he said; he was puzzled by the vast variety of cars of different makes. He said there was so much to see that he couldn't see (this he repeated for several days). And he said he had immediately noticed that in Budapest the air was different. Now he found the air in Vienna different too. We pulled up to the modest Bellevue Hotel; he liked the name and associated it with Tsvetaeva. Together we spent the next few days and nights there ...

Joseph called his parents as soon as we got in and spoke to them for about half an hour. He told me a little about his departure from Leningrad with about 40 people to see him off. The paperwork had cost him $1000, half of it—in true Russian fashion—a fee for losing one's Soviet citizenship! He was allowed to keep $104 after the customs search at Sheremetievo [the Moscow airport]. It had lasted some two hours, while they went over the seams of everything and examined the length of the typewriter ribbon, breaking the paper bail in the process (the old typewriter, I learned, was a gift from Frida Vigdorova). He yelled at them; they said they had a right; he said if so, they should have the technology to manage it. They took away copies of his poems, but he had put off his departure as long as possible in order to have everything typed and microfilmed, and then sent out, he said, with a *Times* correspondent ...

We didn't know then how much trouble holding Joseph's collected works would cause so many people back in Leningrad—Maramzin, Kheifets, Etkind, to name the three who were punished.

We visited the Marksteins that first evening. I didn't know then of her communist past and her friendship with the Kopelevs.

With Mr. Markstein Joseph discussed the matter of his farewell "Letter to Brezhnev," which he told only a little about. He told me it contained some of the same ideas as the letter not sent after the Kuznetsov death verdict. The idea was: Both of us will die one day, you and me. That will be a new thought for him, Joseph said. The time has come when the strong do not always win over the weak, he wrote, and he asked that his name remain in literature, that his parents receive the roughly thousand rubles that were due him for his translation work.

I stress that what I report here is what he told me at the time, as recorded in my daily notes. I have never read the whole text and have not checked it now to see whether the wording is the same. The important thing is what he told of it then, that is how he felt.

Markstein said he should publish the letter, but Joseph said "No, it was a matter between Brezhnev and me." Markstein asked, "And if you publish it, then it's not to Brezhnev?" And Joseph said, yes, precisely.

The Marksteins were very kind, and they offered the services of their young daughters to

show us both around Vienna. But for the most part
we were on our own, and since for the first time
we were spending a great deal of time together
alone, we talked a lot, especially at night.

—Carl Proffer, *Joseph Brodsky:*
Notes for a Memoir, 1984

The shock of arrival converted to anger in Joseph:
as the two men walked around Vienna, Joseph began
spontaneously condemning entire groups of writers
(especially Evtushenko and Voznesensky) and dissidents
in general. These were things he had said before, but
now it was with a kind of hysterical intensity and much
more profanity.

Joseph was overwhelmed, and we would see him like
this in certain situations. He was fine with an audience
because he had a defined role. With groups of people
he didn't know, however, he would revert to a kind of
savage boorishness. As he said himself many times, he
had a kind of emotional claustrophobia. There was also
an element of feeling powerless and embarrassed. That
he and Carl managed to share the same room for these
two weeks is a testament to Joseph's courage and Carl's
patience; it could not have been easy for either of them.

They negotiated, unsuccessfully, with the consulate,
visited various Viennese attractions and then decided to
find Auden. Joseph knew that Auden was still living at
his place in Kirchstetten, an hour from Vienna. Auden
meant a great deal to Joseph, more than any other
poet—this was the sort of poetry Joseph responded to;

his friend Andrei Sergeev had told him that Joseph's poetry reminded him of Auden's, and as soon as he read the English poet, his own poetry reflected that fact. Russian poetry led with emotion, Auden led with restraint, and Joseph immediately found his work inspiring. After the transcript of Joseph's trial was published, Auden translated (from someone's trot) a few poems, then agreed to do the introduction to the forthcoming Penguin *Selected Poems*. Joseph was immensely proud of this connection.

Joseph was bold when he approached the famous and the accomplished. It was not that he was egotistical—although he had a strong ego—it was that he took his calling seriously. This is why he felt he had a right to address Brezhnev—he was a *poet* and therefore equal to any leader. For him being a poet was a gift God had given him, and he meant to honor this talent and behave as a poet should. Some of this attitude may have come from Akhmatova, but he had made it part of his own sense of life. So it was that, as shy as he might be about it, he felt he had a right to approach W. H. Auden. Carl rented a car and drove him to Kirchstetten, where, as Carl wrote, the first contact was disappointing:

> I saw the look of dismay on Auden's face as I approached him; obviously not a few unwanted celebrity-seekers had sought him out in his life, even in this remote abode. As he waved me away and said, "No, I'm busy now," I told him as concisely as I could who I was, who the red-haired

poet behind me was and what extraordinary circumstances had brought the Russian here. He didn't listen, or didn't understand, because he still waved us away like unwanted insects, and Joseph, flushed, pulled me to leave. However, I again made the explanation, in "me-Tarzan-you-Jane" language. Finally, Auden understood it was the Russian Brodsky, whom he had translated and more or less praised.

Now he did invite us in. However, he was at a loss about what to do then. After some mumbling, he offered us some vermouth. (Joseph didn't finish his.) He started blabbing on about "the genius Voznesensky," without listening to Joseph's answer and warnings about being taken in by Voznesensky. After all, Joseph couldn't just say "Voznesensky is shit" as he would normally. Joseph was very frustrated, and even though Auden invited us back Saturday for lunch (his companion would be there), when we drove off down the bumpy lane Joseph growled that it wasn't even worth returning: Auden didn't understand anything. My own return to Michigan precluded my going, but it was extremely unlike Joseph to insult anyone of Auden's stature. He did in fact go back, and obviously he understood that Auden was not a person to be ignored even if he loved Voznesensky's poetry. In any case, as with Akhmatova earlier, the second meeting must have come out better, because in the end Joseph and Auden flew to London on the same plane. In many ways, of course, Auden's patronage was extremely important to Joseph, who was a sincere admirer of the English poet.

—Carl Proffer, *Joseph Brodsky: Notes for a Memoir,* 1984

At this time Joseph could barely speak or understand English, so he required interpreters. Carl was one interpreter, and when he left there were others. (The Russians in Vienna quickly found Joseph and began to help him.) Still, Auden felt his personality, because Joseph ended up staying with him and leaving on the same plane; Joseph tells that story in his essay "To Please a Shadow."

The meeting with Auden, although incredibly important to Joseph, was actually a footnote to the main action for Carl, which was bureaucratic: the consulate had received certain negative information from the Moscow embassy, information which made Joseph seem an undesirable person. There was, for example, information on file that he had planned to enter into a fictitious marriage with an American student—which was, of course, correct.

Joseph was bemused by the fact that the vice-consul, Mr. Segars, was black. Carl was unhappy that the diplomat was barely civil—he was acting dubious that this was a famous poet, dubious that he was worthy of any special attention, dubious that he had a job offer from Michigan.

We knew from our experiences in the Soviet Union that the US diplomatic bureaucracy tended to see tourists—or scholars on an exchange—as nothing more than trouble waiting to happen. Individual diplomats might be understanding and helpful, but in general one did not go to an embassy or consulate seeking good will. Even by these standards the Vienna embassy was a stone wall.

My job in Ann Arbor was to persuade the university people to actually call Segars and inform him that Joseph had already been approved as poet-in-residence for that fall so that he would qualify for "extraordinary status." Worried about this unexpected delay, I began calling all of our journalist and diplomatic friends to get advice on how to get the poet in; I called our friend Bob Kaiser at the *Washington Post*, as well as the Tolstoy Foundation, and told contacts at the *New York Times*. We had all assumed that once Michigan sent its letter documenting Joseph's job offer, things would be easy. However, something or someone had halted the process. I had to keep in contact with the Michigan people to make sure they were following up, sending telegrams to Vienna and so on. And then the media began to influence Joseph's fate. This was an interesting aspect of Joseph's life: he attracted media attention without really trying to.

Hedrick Smith filed his story on June 7, and it appeared in the *New York Times* on June 8: "A Major Poet in Soviet Said to Go to U.S." When I saw that story, I began to feel hopeful, but I had no idea that twenty-six-year-old Strobe Talbott, who worked for *Time* magazine, had already arrived in Vienna from Belgrade after seeing the teletype of the story. Soon after that CBS sent a television team to Vienna, headed by the anchor Peter Kalischer.

Now I began to get calls for information and photos from the country's major papers and magazines, and I began to receive an education in just what publicity can do for a stranded Russian poet. We would need this knowledge in the future to help other writers ...

Details began to change as early as these first stories: OVIR, the passport office, morphed into simply the "secret police," only the beginning of mythologizing that would reach its apogee in the assertion that the KGB had forced Joseph onto his plane.

For Joseph himself this all seemed to be theater. He was still stunned by being out of the Soviet Union, and only dimly understood these negotiations. I think he thought Carl could make anything happen, although that was far from true. Carl himself did not realize that this adamantine bureaucracy could be affected by press attention—but Strobe Talbott did.

Carl reported that Strobe was excellent at dealing both with the reluctant Joseph and the consulate. Carl, Joseph, and he met at a café by the Bristol Hotel. Talbott had a photographer with him named Goess, who was, I think, Viennese. Joseph at this point was getting hostile; he didn't want the press to help him, and he said he wanted to cut the interview short. Strobe, who was both intelligent and persuasive, used every trick he knew to keep Joseph talking. This worked, and the men then went to Goess's apartment, where Strobe planned to make calls to bring pressure on the consulate.

First Strobe talked to the embassy people and artfully induced them to give actual yes or no answers, something they had managed to avoid until then. He told Carl that his experience with government people had made him good at this: to begin with, he always assumed they were lying. (Later Strobe would become a well-known diplomat and undersecretary of state.) At this crucial moment Strobe Talbott was the face of *Time* magazine, then a very influential publication, and his interest made the embassy people understand that Joseph was not someone they could simply force to go on to Israel.

The CBS crew with Peter Kalischer arrived in time to accompany Carl and Joseph on one of their trips to see the vice-consul, supposedly to get a real answer. Kalischer was a classical anchor, constantly checking his hair in a mirror and telling Carl in a moment of manly candor that he hoped the consulate's reply would be negative, "because then it'll be a more interesting show."

Carl was very happy to see the galvanizing effect of a CBS film crew on the heretofore indifferent embassy personnel. They were moved to make vague promises

that some action would be taken, by far the most posi-
tive thing yet to come out of them.

Thanks to Kalischer, Joseph took part in his first tele-
vision show, staged at the magnificent Hotel Palais de
Schwarzenberg. They filmed the poet picturesquely
wandering down a path, reciting his poetry in Russian.
Carl was stunned by the clichéd approach, but it didn't
matter: in the end the tape was never used. It was sent
to the wrong city—Kabul.

The letter from the University of Michigan finally
had its effect, and Carl and Joseph were left to deal
with the most hateful organization of all, the US
Immigration Service, where no matter what the job
offer was, the assumption was always that you were a
criminal and must prove otherwise to gain admittance
to our gleaming democracy.

Carl came back on June 10, leaving Joseph in the
care of the Marksteins and Auden, to face the moun-
tain of paperwork the Department of Labor required
from the university. He and I had to help assemble all
the required materials. For example, it was necessary
to provide documents from other universities declar-
ing what yearly salary they normally paid Russian
poets-in-residence.

Joseph got his visa approved on June 15, and we cel-
ebrated over the phone.

Nadezhda Mandelstam, Moscow, c. 1974.
(Photo: Wayne Robart)

Joseph's parents, Maria and Alexander Brodsky,
Leningrad c. 1974. (Photo: Wayne Robart)

Joseph Brodsky with the Proffer family in his room, Leningrad, 1970. Children, left to right: Christopher, Andrew, Ian.

Joseph Brodsky and Ellendea Proffer, Leningrad, December, 1970.

Left to right: Stephen Spender, John Ashbery, W. H.
Auden, Joseph Brodsky. Poetry festival, London, 1972.

Carl Proffer, Joseph Brodsky, Bert Hornback, on stage
for Brodsky's first public reading in the US.
Rackham Amphitheater, Ann Arbor, September, 1972.

Joseph Brodsky, Carl and Ellendea Proffer.
Mark Hopkins Hotel, San Francisco, 1972.

Joseph Brodsky.
Ann Arbor,
c. 1972.

Carl and Ellendea Proffer, Ann Arbor, c. 1974.
(Photo: Christopher Proffer)

Joseph Brodsky
at Geddes
Lakes,
Ann Arbor,
August 1973.

Brodsky drawing of Proffer, February, 1981.

Brodsky's house in Ann Arbor, 1972.

Brodsky at the Ardis front door during a Michigan snowstorm. Ann Arbor, 1970s.

Brodsky during a Thanksgiving dinner at the Proffers'. Ann Arbor, 1970s.

Proffer and Brodsky at Thanksgiving.

Brosky, Ellendea, Masha Slonim, Vasily Aksyonov. Ann Arbor, 1975.

Brodsky with
Vladimir
Maksimov,
at Ardis, c. 1973.

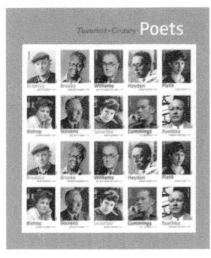

Brodsky on
a sheet of
American
stamps.

Carl, Ellendea Proffer, and Joseph at Ardis, c.1974.

Ann Arbor

On Joseph Brodsky's first morning in the United States, I came downstairs to find a bewildered poet. He held his head with both hands and said: "Everything is surreal."

It was surreal for me as well. Here he was in our little townhouse decorated in seventies style—wall-to-wall carpet, a "Mediterranean" couch, and my mother-in-law's dining set, now used as a conference table.

"I got up this morning," he said, humor mixing with alienation, "and I see Ian sitting on the kitchen counter. He puts bread in a metal box. Then the toast pops up by itself. I don't understand anything."

He had arrived at Detroit Airport the day before, straight from London and his first meetings with famous British poets. And now he was here in Ann Arbor, which in no way corresponded to his imaginings; he really was like that literary frog who woke up and found he was in the Gobi Desert. Like many émigrés, he had imagined this country to be like his minus all the bad things. Nothing could have prepared him for the strangeness of this town, and the place he would occupy in it.

He later said he came to be glad that his start was in Ann Arbor rather than New York, because he had time to adapt and get his English up to speed. Nonetheless, the early days were difficult for him; his eye could not get used to the scale of a university town of a hundred thousand (thirty thousand of them students at the

University of Michigan). Soviet Russia was a centralized universe, with only two cities that mattered. The United States had many centers of power, and some of them looked like this town. He was intelligent enough to understand that he had entered a culture of low context. The only thing unifying the diverse world of Americans was popular culture, and even that was weaker than centrally controlled Soviet propaganda.

Ann Arbor would be Joseph's home base until 1981; he would come back often even after moving away, always warmly welcomed. Joseph complained to Russian friends in the beginning that Ann Arbor was a desert, but actually it was something far, far worse: it was where he was forced to learn many new things, sometimes against his own inclinations. We taught him how to live independently in America—opening a bank account, writing checks, buying food, driving—and it was hard for him, he had no wife or mother to see to these things. All he had was us, and we were both working full-time, so he had to learn quickly.

Teaching Joseph how to drive was a Pninian experience, full of risk and comedy. An epic could be written about the number of people, including Fred Moody, who helped with the driving exam (I think Joseph failed the written test five times); he wanted to cheat, but Carl wouldn't let him—then he was ashamed he had wanted to. He had some spectacular accidents (once he jumped a median strip and ended up facing the wrong way), but he managed not to hurt himself or others.

Ann Arbor was the place he came to the full reali-
zation that he would not see his country again. Joseph
had left his parents behind, and now they were hostages,
one of the many reasons he indulged in no direct polit-
ical activity. (His two children—Andrei Basmanov and
Anastasia Kuznetsova, the daughter of the ballerina
Maria Kuznetsova)—did not have his last name, so they
were somewhat safer.) On one hand, Joseph missed his
family; he was used to living in that tiny room carved
off from theirs. On the other hand, he felt freer than
he ever had in his life. (I recognized him in Bellow's
comment that only in America did the Jewish sons get
to leave their parents' houses.)

He was not cut off from his world in Leningrad:
friends and scholars ferried letters, money, and presents
to them and information and letters back. There was
always someone going or coming, including us, and
there were many friends in Leningrad checking up
on his parents and reporting to Joseph by letter and
telephone.

It took Joseph about six months to people his
Michigan world—Russians found him, American poets
found him, interested graduate students and other
professors found him; he found the girls himself.

He was almost never alone, but he experienced the
loneliness of a man surrounded by people yet aware
that the context has changed. That loneliness had
a special flavor made up of longing and disgust, and
can be seen most prominently in his "Lullaby of Cape
Cod." I know that Joseph had experienced this sort of

loneliness before emigration, but the change sharpened the experience.

The fear that loneliness forced up from his subconscious is most searingly expressed in "The Hawk's Cry in Autumn"; when I read this poem from 1975, I understood that the poet was the hawk who dies because he has flown too high for survival: "what am I doing at such a height?" he asks himself.

Later Joseph gave interviews in which he talked about the years in Michigan as the only childhood he ever had. This is a sad commentary on his real childhood, but it is also a way of acknowledging the safety he felt among so many people willing to help him while respecting his talent. He had a large pool of people he felt at home with: the Ardis editors, who quickly befriended him, and some of his university colleagues and students.

His new profession was a challenge: Joseph had never gone to regular classes, he had sat in on a few lectures and seminars in Leningrad—so he had no concept of what undergraduate teaching might be, never mind in an American university. The American educational system differed profoundly from the Soviet one in that rote memorization was not emphasized and in that specialization did not really begin until the last two years of college. Therefore some of Joseph's students were majoring in other fields and had no background in literature. He assumed that they were stupid. These students were young—nineteen or twenty—and were not used to openly expressed contempt from their professors.

Some of the students complained to Carl that Joseph would read them poems in English and they could not understand a word because of his accent. For all that, most of them stayed, compelled by his personality and by the idea that you might learn something different from him. He was an uneven teacher: in the first years he did not really prepare and relied on being better informed than his students, at least about the small selection of poets he was teaching. Sometimes he hit a smart undergraduate, but if they got too philosophical he made fun of them. When a student gave him the answer he wanted, he was warm and enthusiastic.

Teaching and socializing with young Americans was how Joseph's spoken English improved; if he had taught in Russian, this would never have happened, and Carl was very aware of that, and of the fact that Joseph had to have a certain number of students to keep his job. While it is true that an exceptional person such as Joseph will always find help, it is also true that he was lucky that the help was coming from someone as gifted as Carl, who knew how to navigate a university.

Teaching was paying Joseph's bills, but he did not take it very seriously, especially at the start, because it was so strange to find himself in such a position. He was nominated for many grants, and got them—a Guggenheim, a MacArthur Fellowship, and so on—but his steady job from 1972 until his death was teaching. He did not always do it conscientiously. Susan Sontag saw him enter a classroom unprepared and winging it; others reported that he arrived smelling of strong spirits.

He liked to stack the deck, having students read a weak Yeats poem and then a strong Auden poem, to demonstrate who was better. His wide knowledge of poetry and the intensity of his dedication carried him through even the bad times. He was an example of something these students rarely encountered, a poetic genius, thinking out loud.

We saw Joseph daily, usually for supper, and he seemed energetic and upbeat, no matter what was going on. As always, his sense of humor got him through a lot of difficult moments. Joseph's conversation would begin with ideas and then quickly shift into gossip, as it tends to do with writers. Joseph was a funny gossip, laughing his way through the stories he heard about his friends in New York, such as the dramatic evolution of an affair between two writers we knew, featuring incredible drunkenness and the screaming of love poetry in public places. He was kept informed by phone almost daily about these events … He knew how to tell a funny story, expressing delighted astonishment at human absurdity.

He never wanted anyone to gossip about him, of course, and he made a point of that. Once he gave me his usual high-minded speech about poets: all that matters is the poetry, nothing else. (This from a man who read everything he could about other poets and their lives and liked to repeat the famous line about preferring the perfection of the work to the perfection of the life.) I responded that now we wanted to know absolutely everything about Pushkin and that when you loved a poet an interest in his life naturally followed.

Carl arranged for Joseph to write a long essay for the *New York Times*, an essay filled with flailing attempts at significance and coherence, but containing the first printed statement of the poet's credo: man is radically evil by nature, and political movements are merely a way to avoid personal responsibility for what is happening, a way to think one is good, a kind of rationalization; change must come from within, as a man feels shame and takes a good look at himself.

While a Soviet Russian had every reason to dislike political parties, an American could be forgiven for wondering why this was an either/or proposition, that one couldn't be a member of a political group and also a good person.

Joseph understood that this essay was important for his future, but for a long time he was casual about his prose, which is part of the reason why he let people edit and rewrite his essays to correct the English: it wasn't poetry, after all. It was a way to work out his ideas, and that was what interested him. Gradually he began to realize that prose was a way to reach a wider audience and build a reputation, but even then he was tolerant of editorial changes that he would not have accepted in translations of his poetry.

This first essay was followed about a year later by our friend Arthur A. Cohen's influential evaluation of Joseph as a poet in the same publication. These events signaled Joseph's arrival to those in the literary world who had not paid attention up till then, and they had the desired effect of making that world take him seriously.

Joseph's literary rise, which can only be compared to T. S. Eliot's in London, began immediately with important contacts in New York. Joseph's biography played a role, certainly, but his personality and intelligence counted for even more. His early essays may not have had the polish—or the coherence—of his best-known ones, but his intellectual force was already striking. It did not hurt that he had knowledge of English-language poets and that he was interested in the same European material that American writers found compelling. He was, however, an enemy to the avant-garde, which was both an esthetic and a political position in his case. He saw the avant-garde as a tool of the young Soviet regime. For him the radical position was the traditional position. In many ways his ideas about literature and art were old-fashioned to the American sensibility, but his personality and passion made them feel new.

I look back at all the new things this poet had to do and I see Joseph's courage, his openness to challenges, his ability to pull up his socks. He was a fast learner, and he got independent of us as soon as he possibly could. It was very important that we had known him in his Russian life—otherwise we would not have understood many things. It was equally important that he have a sample of somewhat ordinary American life and that Carl be his guide. Carl was a full-time professor, a publisher, and the father of three sons, but he somehow found the time to get Joseph through the most difficult tests of his new world.

There were limits to our understanding, however—this was the first Russian émigré in our intimate life, and we had not anticipated some of the difficulties a Soviet Russian would have in our culture.

Joseph arrived as a special person, in special circumstances, but he was shocked at the almost invisible status of a poet in the United States. He was determined to change all that. We were witness to how precisely the Brodskyan *roman de réussite* was managed. Joseph's aggressive individualism was in direct opposition to the degrading of humanism in the Soviet system of the triumph of the state, the supposed deification of the working class. In the West, however, Joseph would have an opportunity to construct a career, which he did to a degree unusual even for gifted émigrés.

He quickly learned who mattered and who didn't; in any case Carl had already set up a number of contacts, as had George Kline and, of course, Auden. Joseph's emotional intelligence was crucial in the formation of his career. He quickly figured out who could be kept waiting and who could not; he knew how to be interesting to interesting people, and for the most part he avoided offending those who were powerful. This last was difficult for him, because he was used to saying exactly what he thought in the Russian context; however he quickly understood that he had to show more self-control in this new environment. Sometimes he couldn't manage it, and we would receive reports of nasty insolence directed at professors who had invited him to come to their universities to speak.

Joseph accepted almost all invitations to write essays for major publications, to take part in literary events, to give readings, and to give lectures. This was an entire career in itself in terms of time and energy expended, but it was his instinct—and his nature—to say yes, to be open to everything. His biography, of course, preceded him, and once at a new place he would be engaging and would therefore make new friends.

Carl, who was only forty-six and facing death as he wrote his notes for a memoir about Joseph, saw a touch of careerism and mythmaking in Joseph's behavior with the people who mattered. From my point of view Joseph was doing what was natural to him, and what was natural to him was to make connections and increase his fame. For a Russian intellectual to openly admit to wanting fame was almost shameful, but Joseph was his own man in this as in so many other areas. If you had fame, you had the power to affect a culture; if you had fame, you were showing the Soviets what they had lost.

Joseph Brodsky was very proud of being a poet, of having received this gift from God, and for most of his life writing was joy. I do not remember him complaining about being blocked. He liked writing in cozy spaces reminiscent of his Leningrad room, and the minute he had a good line he wanted to read it to you. Sometimes he would be talking with us as a solution to a line presented itself, and he would go off and write it. Creation was his element; but creation is not the same as publication.

As his Russian-language publishers, we were surprised at how difficult it was to get him to assemble the poems for a book—it reminded me of the stories about the nineteenth-century poet Lermontov. There was some essential reluctance to have the poems become a book. Usually someone else had to gather together the poems previously published separately in journals, and then he would start getting interested—changing the order, writing entirely new poems. If not for Vladimir Maramzin, who assembled a five-volume samizdat edition in 1974 and was then arrested for it (Carl and Joseph mounted a campaign to free him), the Russian reader would have lost a great deal of the early work. Despite the fact that for many readers the early work was the most loved, Joseph regarded it all as juvenilia and would have destroyed it if he could have. He was right in thinking the early work had many imperfections; his ambition was outstripping his technical abilities almost to the point of incoherence. But that incoherence had genius in it.

His first two Ardis books came out only in 1974, when his friend Lev Lifshits (later Losev) worked at Ardis and managed to drag the poems out of him. Joseph demanded control over the design, going so far as to draw the lion on the depressing gray covers. The books were not attractive, which everyone noticed, and later he was happy when I redesigned the covers of all his books to make them uniform. Nonetheless, this first experience of shepherding his book through press was exciting to him. He could not forget that his poet friends back home could not get anything published, never mind a book, and in a sense he felt guilty that it was so easy for him. He was highly competitive, although not with his friends; but, of course, none of them were on his level, and he knew that.

Joseph's tendency to see things purely from his own point of view and his need to bend the world to that view had a negative effect on the translations of his own poetry. Much depended on these translations, as Carl and I knew, and only a few of the first ones were really good, such as those by Wilbur and Updike. Others, by George Kline and Carl himself, were workmanlike, but the poetic voice was sometimes missing. Joseph wanted rhymed translations, preferably ones retaining the metrics of the original; this was not possible when translating from an inflected language into an uninflected one. In Russia Joseph had done many translations from many languages, working from literal translations done by native speakers. He considered himself an expert translator because of this work.

The translation wars were carried on, at tedious length, by telephone, at the table in our Ann Arbor house, and later in New York cafes. As I remember those arguments, ennui sets in. I don't really want to write about this; I lived through it once and that was enough, but since it had such an influence on Joseph's reputation as a poet in English, I feel I must.

What Joseph was trying to do, few would have hazarded, and we were dismayed. Boldness and confidence had been the marks of his happy career, but here these excellent qualities were in the service of hubris, if not delusion. Many, many poets and scholars told Joseph that his work would suffer in a rhymed translation, that the poetic thought structure would be deformed in order to get the rhyme, and so on.

The English Joseph heard in his head had a Russian intonation. Americans told him he had very good English, but no one ever said that he had no accent. (In general he was unaware of American politeness and did not know, for example, that when people were silent it did not necessarily mean assent.) When he first came to live in Ann Arbor, he concluded that Americans had no slang. Joseph, I explained to him, we all speak to you in normal English so that you will understand. You wouldn't understand it if we spoke in slang, and we know that.

He perfected his English at fantastic speed and started studying rhyming dictionaries and dictionaries of slang. However, and this is in no way odd, he could not feel the appropriateness of a word, given its normal and historical usage; he was limited to what a dictionary gave as examples.

Joseph's attitude from the beginning was that of a literary Cortez: in his stated views, contemporary American poets were weak in that many of them had given up rhyme, and they had done that because they just didn't know how to find new rhymes. He would accept no other explanations—to write poetry without rhyme was to play tennis without a net. He would translate himself and show how it should be done.

Translation was something mystical for Joseph. He had absorbed many literatures in translation, but he was a very unusual reader. He used to say that if he read the first lines of a poem in an original language, he could guess how it would end. He is on record as saying that Cavafy may be said to have actually *gained* in translation—but how would anyone who did not know Greek be able to say such a thing?

This was a man who had Carl and then others correct his English spelling and grammar before sending anything on to an editor, yet he saw no problem in taking on the challenge of translating himself. Everyone close to him, and many were poets, advised him not to do this, especially when he showed his first attempts.

In this period the battle between Nabokov and Wilson over Nabokov's very literal translation of Pushkin's *Onegin* was causing the kind of acrimony last seen during the Dreyfus case. Carl was in general on Nabokov's side, but he saw that Nabokov's translation could not stand alone: the commentary was an essential part of the project. Very few readers—or publishers—could tolerate this level of scholarly meticulousness.

I took the middle position: I did not want metaphors changed at will. I wanted to see, for example, just how Mandelstam developed his imagery in "The Horseshoe Finder," and if you could give me rhyme and meter along with that, God grant you a Bollingen

Prize. For me, however, knowing what the poet had actually said mattered.

As literary people, and translators ourselves, we understood that a translation could never convey all the music of the original. The aim was to reach a state of tolerable dissatisfaction ... Pound's translation of Li Po's "Exile's Letter," for example, seemed to me to take unconscionable liberties. Into the monochromatic system of the Chinese poem he had introduced the exciting adjective "vermilion," and now that was what everyone who read only English remembered about the poem.

This did not bother Joseph at all. He would sacrifice a great deal to get that meter and rhyme, and if he had been bilingual, perhaps it would have worked. Joseph was not only not bilingual; he did not sense the stresses and pitch in the English phrases, which meant that even technically correct lines came out sounding strange or like doggerel. Complex sentences sometimes ended up not making sense, which in Russian would not have mattered, but in English it did.

Joseph very much wanted the other major poets— his only peers—to be able to see what his poetry was really like, and he worked very hard to show them ...

As time went on, he got better at translating his poems, but not before he had disenchanted serious readers of poetry. Friends of mine—American poets or Russian scholars—would call me up and sadistically read the latest Brodsky translation (or English original), and I got very tired of defensively saying that he was a great poet in Russian.

People ask why his translations were not seriously criticized until after his death. The answer is that he was both influential and vengeful, and therefore some felt the cost of giving an honest evaluation was too high. As for his friends, poets and otherwise, they loved him and they did not want to hurt his feelings. Sometimes a reputation overwhelms reality: Joseph could be wonderful in conversation; he was genuinely serious about culture and knowledgeable about poetry. How could he not be a great translator of himself? In addition—and this is always a point where Joseph is concerned—his poetic biography of persecution by a totalitarian state gave him immunity from the normal literary process both in America and Britain, at least in print.

Joseph had taken over the translation of his own work fairly early, but as the years passed he actually began to compose poems in English. The reasons for this are complex, and I know only a few of them. When he wrote the moving essay about his parents in *Less Than One*, he made the point that he was writing about them in English to grant them some sense of freedom, because writing in Russian would further their captivity. This is part of the reason he would give readings of his poetry in Boston in English rather than Russian in front of a mostly Russian audience. It is also true that Joseph's close friends were now some of the most eminent of the English-language poets and he wanted to belong to their guild. He denied in one interview that he wanted to become an American poet, but as I look back, I think that is precisely what he was working toward, and in part this is connected to his sense of rejection by his own culture.

In both his life and his work Joseph occasionally expressed guilt and self-disgust, but never in relation to his gift, the most important fact of his existence. I took him as a force of nature and did not really think about how his identity was tied to his work until one night when we were being silly together.

It was late in the evening, sometime in 1973, after we had moved our family and publishing company into an old country club, a house big enough to store our books now that Ardis was expanding. Joseph and I were alone at the butcher-block table in the kitchen. The children had left a pair of toy lie detector cuffs on the table. This was a primitive device to measure blood pressure changes, but Joseph was intrigued. Let's try them, he said. He put them on me and with a triumphant look asked me if I engaged in a certain solitary sexual activity. I said yes: the needle jumped about halfway.

I was not expecting this sort of question, but I immediately knew what my question would be. I put the cuffs on him and asked: Do you think you are a great poet?

Yes, he said. He blushed, and the needle jumped almost all the way. It was the blush that was so endearing.

I should have understood everything in that moment—why he destroyed himself smoking, why he refused to take care of his body—but I didn't; I was still young, I thought people could change when their life was on the line.

He had worked in a morgue, he knew what real death was like, and he had great fear of it—terror, actually. In his poems he portrays a man who is impassive in the face of the certain death that comes to us all, but that is not how he lived.

A striking Ann Arbor moment comes back to me as I write this. In January 1980 we took Joseph to see Fosse's *All That Jazz*. Joseph was deeply affected by movies because he was so open to the visual and the emotional. This movie portrays the life of a self-destructive, womanizing choreographer who is burning himself out, and smoking constantly despite warnings that he has a bad heart. In the center of this knowing musical was a very realistic open-heart operation, of the kind Joseph had had himself. As those scenes came up, I looked over at Joseph and he was gripping the sides of the seat.

Afterwards he just said, "It was a very interesting personal experience."

Much, much later, when he had had his second bypass surgery and I angrily asked why he continued to smoke, that it was a form of suicide, he answered: If I don't smoke, I can't write.

The Muse and the Addressee

It is litotes to say that Joseph had trouble with women; they were a sport and a pastime, certainly, but occasionally they were the possibility of love. He was impossible in every way a man can be impossible in matters of love and sex, and he was far from believing that in seductions begin responsibilities. When he was attracted to a woman, he was in the moment and he would say or do anything to seduce her, and sometimes he may have even believed what he was saying—but I don't think so. He would usually begin by arousing sympathy for his tragic position, mentioning prison and exile and the wife and child left behind. For some women this intense focus on the part of a brilliant, charming man was enough. One of them said to me: "What could I do? He wanted it so much."

He was intensely possessive and jealous, as well as unrealistic. He would leave a woman for half a year and then come back to her and be surprised that she had gotten married in the meantime. He would describe it as a rejection.

His attitude was that any attractive woman was fair game, even if she was married to a friend. The idea was that esthetics ruled all and creativity was closely connected to sexuality, plus the erotic is the antidote to the fear of death, and so forth. This all sounds typical of literary bohemia until you get to the vast, exploitable category of undergraduate girls who were harvested like a crop. In his view, the young girls knew what they were getting into—and if they didn't, high time they learned.

This subject brought out his worldly, cynical, and pitiless side. He was happily hypocritical about all this, condemning his married friends for having affairs while he himself seduced married women. He was romantically reckless. He came back from a visit to Rome once and gave me a comic summary: there I am, in a private Roman garden, being chased by the count because I'd been with the countess ...

There were the women of a day, a month, or a year. But there was only one woman of his poetry. Marina Basmanova looked like the Swedish actress Joseph imprinted on early in his teens. Marina, an artist from an eccentric family of artists, was as difficult as he was.

They were very young, and the romance was marked by lots of breakups and makeups. When he was in trouble with the authorities, Marina began a romance with his best friend, explaining that she and Joseph were over. Joseph heard about this immediately and almost lost his mind. He told me that during this dangerous period he was more worried about his romantic problems than his prison ones. I believe him, because despite his great intelligence his emotions dominated him. Marina got pregnant, had the child, and left Joseph a final time. In certain ways Joseph was conventional, and I think it was beyond his imaginings that she would do this after they had a child. (He hinted to me once that he had gotten her pregnant as a way of keeping her, but I don't know if that was true; there is, however, a line in one his poems to this effect.) He was certainly a person who valued most what was being denied him, and Marina's power was greatest when she exhibited her independence.

Once when Marina had broken with him, Joseph told me he cut one of his wrists, then thought better of it, and walked around all day with a bleeding bandaged wrist in his pocket. It may be that for his sort of personality after the first love there is no other. He later referred to this period as "melodrama," but I have more sympathy for the devastated young poet than he did. He felt that this girl was his fate and to lose her was to lose love itself.

Marina was strange, Joseph said, he knew that; but he himself felt strange so he thought they made a couple. He was marked for life by this woman—or perhaps the idea of her—his art powered by the sense of lost love and longing. She was an art-school girl—like Lily Brik and Nadezhda Mandelstam—with a mind of her own. She was complex and unpredictable, and he couldn't get his way with her. She kept her mystery and defied Joseph's need for control, which just made her even more important to him. It was never going to work, given Joseph's compulsive infidelity, but the idea of a happy love that might have been haunted him.

I don't agree with the general view that Marina was to blame for everything. As I think about Joseph's sensitivity to rejection and his extreme jealousy, I wonder about his early life, when he had his mother all to himself while his father was first at war and then serving in China. That father left when Joseph was two and came back when he was eight. It is possible that at that point Joseph experienced some loss of maternal love, as Maria Moiseevna got her husband back. Her son was certainly no longer her singular focus, and his father, the military man, started to discipline the boy.

Marina Basmanova was not only his muse, in the sense of inspiring poems over almost thirty years, she was also the addressee. I often sensed the presence of Marina in the poet's thought even if a poem was dedicated to someone else. She was often the imagined reader, and she knew it; as will be seen, she read his poetry attentively long after he had left Leningrad.

In the early years of our friendship, Marina's name came up a great deal in Joseph's conversation. In 1971, when we were with him for New Year's Eve, Carl asked him what the most important thing Joseph did not know was (a very Carlovian question).

At first Joseph answered jokingly: "When the second coming is."

His second answer was honest: "Where my first wife is at this moment ... But why I should care after so long a time—that's the real mystery."

Two or three years later in Ann Arbor, he started talking with me about why she wouldn't stay with him. Joseph tried very hard to be discreet and to compartmentalize relationships, but his emotional needs of the moment tended to win out over these aspirations. "She told me that I was raping her mind," he said, bewildered.

I knew what she meant. Joseph was intensely categorical in his opinions, and you could feel battered by the force of them. He didn't mean it to be taken that way, but that is how it felt sometimes, especially when he was in free flow. And by his account Marina was a person of silences; she couldn't get away from the power of his personality, the noise of his speech.

Marina herself kept in touch with Joseph off and on and reportedly read his letters with great interest: I got the sense that there would always be something between these two.

Joseph had done his best to prejudice us against her, but at the same time he wanted us to admire her, saying she was a very good artist. As he put it in one of his poems, she had taught him to see.

Periodically Joseph was attracted to women of quality, the kind who require fidelity. When the inevitable bad quarter of an hour came, he seemed to be surprised and bewildered that they didn't see things the way he did. These women, much like Marina, were both intelligent and beautiful, and he couldn't or wouldn't keep them.

It seemed to me that the real issues were his emotional claustrophobia and that he never stopped feeling married to Marina—until she herself got married. He kept tabs on her and received reports from various people in Leningrad who knew that he had a need to know not just about his son but also about his son's mother.

She—or the idea of her—had fantastic power over him for most of his life, and I think the following story from Carl's notes demonstrates that. It is something straight out of F. Scott Fitzgerald's life.

> One evening in October 1981 Joseph called me and said he was going to try to get married!

Joseph was at some important political meeting in Canada, and there, 48 hours earlier, he had seen a woman who was exactly the image of Marina. He was stunned. He was as if in a dream, the sense of reincarnation was so great, as she walked toward him at the hotel. And then it transpired that she was a journalist, partly Dutch, partly Jewish, and one of her plans was to interview Joseph for Dutch radio.

He turned on all the charm at his command, and though there were some things about her that didn't fit, he won her over. I asked him if he had asked her already and he said: "I voiced the idea. She was not terribly against it."

But she was on her way back to Holland, so he would follow.

"It may or may not happen," he said. Had he told her why he was attracted to her in the first place? No, he hadn't. He just kept saying to me "Carl, isn't it very strange, I am slightly out of my mind, I think."

All I could do was wish him luck and suggest caution. He wasn't rational, and he knew it. He followed the replica of Marina to the Netherlands, pressed his suit, as they used to say, but ran into a series of major and minor nightmares, ranging from her abhorrent (to him) left-wing politics and art to a previous and still present lover (the details were suited to the basic plot). After a fairly short period of time it looked like marriage was not to be, but Joseph was very unwilling to completely abandon the notion, and he came back, exhausted and angry, but also still somehow enthralled. I think more by the idea, the Marina in it all, than by the reality.

This story illustrates the incredible power that even the idea of Marina had on Joseph (and how he believed one person could really replace another exactly), something that anyone who undertakes an analysis of his books should take into account.

—Carl Proffer, *Joseph Brodsky:*
Notes for a Memoir, 1984

Over the years we published all of Joseph's major books of poetry, and, of course, we noticed that many separate poems were connected to Marina. It was not until 1983, when we were putting together the Russian edition of *New Stanzas to Augusta* (a collection of all the poems connected to her), that the scale of his project emerged—because, I think, it only became clear to him at that time. Poems that had been dedicated to other loves were swept into this collection as the poet calmly explained that they had been "really" written about or for Marina.

The title, *New Stanzas to Augusta*, made no sense to me. Byron's poems to his sister are touching—he sees Augusta as the only person who really loves him as the scandal that will send him abroad is breaking around him. Once again an English-language poet—the most famous of all—is the Russian poet's reference point.

Marina's position in his life, however, most closely matches that of Byron's wife, Annabella, who rejected the English poet as mad after a year of marriage and left, taking with her the daughter he would never see again. Byron wrote some poems about this wife, and they do share some themes with Joseph.

Joseph wrote the original cycle in September 1964, during his exile in Norenskaia, and now he saw that many poems from different periods really belonged together, forming a novel in verse.

After *New Stanzas to Augusta* came out, Joseph called and told Carl that Marina, who had been out of touch for a long time, had just called him to discuss the book. Remarkably, it was a long, civil conversation in which she told him what she liked and didn't like about the collection dedicated to her.

Carl was amazed. "I imagine," he wrote, "that there have been few cases in world literature where the Muse, particularly such a difficult one, suddenly materialized in this way to reward the poet who sang her."

The Oldest Modern City

One night after Joseph moved to his little apartment on Morton Street in Greenwich Village, he awoke in the middle of the night: a thief was standing in his bedroom.

"Who are you?" Joseph asked him.

"Who are *you*?" The thief asked.

"I'm just a Russian poet."

Then the thief quickly left.

Joseph called us the next day, and he was both shocked and exhilarated. I don't remember what year it was, but it seems to me that it was during his first few years in the city.

It is telling that Joseph's poetry contains few references to his time in Ann Arbor—nine years—or to his time in New York, which was his true home for the rest of his life. He loved England, he loved Italy, he loved Poland—he loved many places he traveled, and he could have had permanent jobs in any of those places, but he stayed in New York, partly because only the United States was the anti-Soviet Union he required, but in great measure because of the way you can be both lost and found in Manhattan. One minute you are the famous poet visiting PEN (I was with him on one of those visits, and masculine competition coated the walls with testosterone), the next you are anonymous in the crowd. Ann Arbor was a town; Leningrad was a small city; New York City was an entire irreducible world.

He had taught off and on in New York, but I count him as a real New Yorker from 1977, the moment he rented his apartment on Morton Street. He knew some of the people already renting in this little building, and the landlord was Andrew Blane, a professor of Russian history. This was a congenial environment and not at all lonely, unless you wanted it to be.

In 1981 he got an appointment as professor at the Five Colleges (Mount Holyoke, etc.), and lived in South Hadley, Massachusetts, during the semester he taught.

New York suited him; he loved it like the city boy he was. He did not take advantage of all its possibilities: in theory he was interested in concerts, art exhibits, movies, and theater, but he rarely went to such things voluntarily. Music, I think, was something private for him, so he chose records over sitting with a group of unknown people. An enormous amount of his time in the city was taken up with meeting friends and having rendezvous with women. When he was teaching in South Hadley, his life was less frenetic, and he probably wrote more, although I remember sometimes he would just stay up all night in New York to get work done, usually after the third deadline had come and gone.

New York and fame are a tricky combination. It took him a while to find his own key. At first everything was in the key of Auden. At times he would seem to be imitating Auden, verbally as well as gesturally. He had always been very attentive to his clothes, and they were never chosen at random, so when I met him for lunch in the Village early in the New York years and he was dressed in a tattered Harris tweed jacket with stains and holes all over it, I understood this was his homage to Auden, an attempt to seem humble. I told him he had gone too far with the professorial indifference and now looked like a homeless person. He made a face, but the next time I saw him he looked normal. But he got his own back: he looked at my coat and boots and said I looked very midwestern—not, of course, a compliment.

Here, in the opposing empire, he was not only accepted, but he had influence, he became part of the establishment. There were some unpleasant consequences for him when Russians from both the emigration and the Soviet Union came to him for help getting published. He tried to be kind and generous, but after a while he simply got tired of the demands. "These people don't understand my life here," he would say, and he was right. Old friends were stung by his patronizing remarks; he was behaving as if he was above his company. His particular code led him to agree to write introductions for the books of friends and then complain that he had been forced into it. This made me wonder what he said about us in such moods.

In the Soviet Union Joseph Brodsky had been known only to inside literary people. Now he had power, and he had trouble getting the balance right. There were moments when Joseph was almost as pompous as Gore Vidal, the gold standard in this area. He would say things like "my humble self," and there was not enough irony in the world to defuse it. We were very busy publishing, writing, and teaching—not to mention going to Russia—but he wanted us to have more famous friends, commenting that ours were too ordinary. A little of this went a long way, although I knew he was just trying to bring us up to his level of fame …

Once we were all in Chicago for a conference, along with Stephen Spender, and I got to see Joseph's behavior with someone who really mattered to him. It was painful: he was not himself and was engaged in a performance. Spender, a quite beautiful old man, handled it well, but we were surprised that Joseph was still so uncomfortable with him.

Our house and our company became part of Joseph's possessions, and he disposed of them as he saw fit. When Masha Slonim and her son had just arrived in New York, he saw that they needed a place to stay and sent them to us. We had known Masha in Moscow and liked her, so that rescue was fine. Other people he sent us didn't work out as well ("Carl," he said, "I've never asked anything of you, just please hire this man ...") but usually Carl was able to arrange for them to go to graduate school, and some ended up as professors.

Joseph came back to Ann Arbor often, sometimes accompanied by New York friends such as Mikhail Baryshnikov, who was extremely charming and always a good friend to Joseph. I think that this friendship was more important than many others. Joseph felt understood by Baryshnikov and could relax with him. Misha was unbelievably famous, and he did not need anything from Joseph. Baryshnikov had spent his formative years in Leningrad and was now part of the dance establishment in New York. It seemed to me that they understood each other well.

Another visitor was Baryshnikov's and Joseph's friend, Gennady Smakov, a man we had known in Leningrad as well. Gena, as he was known, was a remarkable blend of abilities: he had a degree in classics and was an expert on both ballet and literature. He had known Joseph well and told me that Joseph in the early work was prone to get the details of a myth wrong, but that what mattered with him was the stream of words itself.

Joseph brought some lovely, accomplished women to Ann Arbor. I remember Linda Gregg, the poet, a lovely blonde, and Barbara Sproul—a professor, tall, dark, and equal to anything. Joseph and Barbara had just returned from Mexico.

"How did you like Mexico?" Barbara was asked.

"I didn't see Mexico so much as I saw *Joseph* in Mexico," she said, with the humor of a woman who understood writers.

Joseph made it clear to us that these, and others, were romantic relationships. When he brought Susan Sontag to the house, however, his first words to me were in Russian: *eto ne te veshchi* (it's not that sort of thing), emphasizing that this was a friendship, nothing more. It changed key later, but he never mentioned that, he just assumed that we knew it had. Joseph's first heart attack in New York came the day he was helping Susan move. Always macho, he insisted on carrying heavy boxes up stairs when he was in no shape to do so.

Susan—tall, beautiful, and famous—was certainly his type. When he talked to me about her, he disparaged her short stories, precisely as a New York insider would. "Ellendea, I don't know why she keeps writing them," he said, in the same distressed tone we ourselves used about his translations.

That Susan and Joseph would be attracted was predictable; they both were in love with European culture (while not being European themselves, an important point) and with the literature of ideas. They came to the Europe of the intellect from very different viewpoints, of course. Sontag, no enemy of the avant-garde, was aware of the range of American culture, while Joseph was not. She was also a person who read every word of the books she talked about.

Joseph's love of European culture (always excepting France) was not only natural to him as a child of Petersburg, it was part of the ongoing Russian argument between the Slavophiles (Solzhenitsyn) and the Westernizers (Pushkin, Mandelstam). Therefore his poetry carried extra meaning for a Russian reader, especially one who had not traveled. The poet traveled for his readership in a sense. Of course, what is missing from this historic argument about whether Russia should be part of Europe or go its own "organic" way is the United States, with its almost terrifyingly syncretic attitudes and practices. As for Asia, excepting a few very famous, centuries-dead literary figures, it seemed to him an undifferentiated mass of fatalism. Every time

Joseph talked about the number killed under Stalin he assumed that the Soviet people had won the Olympics of suffering; China didn't exist. For this Westernizer, the Asiatic sensibility was the enemy.

Joseph had a transformative effect on the minority of intellectuals who had persisted in believing that Communism was a positive path for humanity. The majority of the leftist intellectuals had been dis-illusioned at the time of the Hitler-Stalin pact, and the Soviet suppression of Hungary and then Czechoslovakia had only confirmed these attitudes. A sense persisted in people of feeling and thought that capitalism was brutal and not everything about the Russian Revolution was bad. Joseph had no interest in nuanced thinking on this subject; he was persuasive in expressing his overwhelming disgust at how his coun-try had been enslaved, and he considered all Marxists agents of such slavery.

Like all totalitarian regimes, the Soviet system required not just obedience but complicity, and this Joseph steadfastly refused to provide. In America self-betrayal could take a different form. For example, Joseph defended the murderer-generals of Argentina on the grounds that any country could be hijacked by a communist party, and the good of the many trumped the deaths of a few. This attitude revealed a lack of understanding of the specifics that stand behind gener-alizations. If he had spent time with Jacobo Timerman, as Carl and I did, he would no doubt have come to understand the problem of using evil to fight evil. The Argentine author of *Prisoner without a Name, Cell without a Number*, tortured and then imprisoned under the Argentine generals (because he began publishing the names of the "disappeared" in his newspaper), had much in common with the Russian poet.

Joseph's prejudice against anything he perceived as politically anti-American made him blind to this country's nonconformists, who resisted much and obeyed little. Since everything was fed into his schema of "if it's against the Soviets, I'm for it," Joseph could not begin to see how much he had in common with the American skeptics.

Because they were anti-Soviet, Joseph seemed attracted to the establishment, political as well as literary. He enjoyed going to President George H. W. Bush's White House dinner; he liked being close to power.

This Russian was attractive to the American poets for many reasons, not least his belief that being a poet was the highest calling there could be. He lived this and he preached it, and the American poets, feeling the smallness of their audience and often lost in the academic maze, were energized by such passion. Of the poets, he admired Richard Wilbur and had warm personal friendships with Anthony Hecht, Derek Walcott, and Seamus Heaney.

The influence went both ways: Joseph was educated and changed by all these brilliant people. He began to mention positively literary figures he formerly would not have considered important—Elizabeth Bishop, Simone Weil, and Walter Benjamin, for example—

and to read writers he would never have known about otherwise.

Joseph moved in many different circles, charming and becoming intimate with other writers, people in the worlds of fashion and ballet, and, of course, publishing. He was proud and possessive of his relations with the famous; if we had our own encounters with such people, he was always at pains to show that he knew them better—and usually he did. We learned not to talk about the famous people we were seeing in Russia because it always upset him in some way.

If there was ever a group Joseph had a strong negative reaction to, it was the literary stars of his era, especially Evtushenko, Akhmadulina, and Voznesensky. These people were incredibly famous in Russia—read, adored, known in a way that Joseph was not. A poet in Russia is given the significance of a law-giver, something almost sacred. Joseph was infuriated by the fame of these poets. It can safely be conjectured that he was envious, that he wanted to be famous in his homeland in that way, but his hostility was also based on the conviction that these people were political puppets. Despite these feelings, Joseph had agreed to give readings with these stars after his trial, an invitation meant to grant him a sort of protection. He was not grateful.

Joseph considered that he understood most people well, and that understanding led to forgiveness—but these famous figures were never given forgiveness.

So it was a distressed Joseph who called Carl in the summer of 1977 when *Vogue* commissioned an article on Bella Akhmadulina, who was visiting New York at the time. He cursed himself for having taken on the job and said he couldn't turn down the money, but Carl thought what he couldn't turn down was having his name in *Vogue* (*Vogue's* literary pieces were noticed and carried a certain prestige). I am not so sure. Joseph had trouble saying no in general (hence contradictory promises to publishers, including us).

Bella Akhmadulina, a fine poet and a very decent person, was someone we knew and liked, so it was hard to listen to Joseph somewhat hysterically run her down. She was in no way a compromiser—her sin, other than being famous, was being an ex-wife of Evtushenko. Since Joseph conceived of everything as a test of ethics, the obvious question was what was he doing writing about her? He was uncomfortable with himself about this.

Carl could occasionally reframe situations so that Joseph could justify changing his direction on a difficult subject; this time Carl said very little because he was too angry.

After Joseph spent time with Bella, he called to report something unexpected to us: he himself was affected by her peculiar glamour.

"I don't understand what happened to me," he said.

My guess is that he was affected by her personality, which was elemental and essentially reserved, and that when he was with her, his inner opposition dissolved.

The article in *Vogue*, of course, was very flattering, and he was not proud of it. It turned out that Bella had heard what he really thought of her work, yet she never let that affect her very high evaluation of his work. She was the sort of person who does not speak evil of others but knows precisely what they have said of her.

The idea that you could compromise your integrity outside of the Soviet system continued to be something Joseph was blind to, and his behavior to our friend Vasya (Vasily) Aksyonov caused one of our most serious disagreements with Joseph.

Aksyonov, the son of Evgeniia Ginsburg (who wrote a famous book about her journey through Stalin's camp system), was the most popular prose writer of these years. His books sold out in hours, and his effect on the readers of his time can only be compared to the Dos Passos of *Manhattan Transfer* and the Salinger of *The Catcher in the Rye*. Aksyonov was generous to other writers and tolerant of their eccentricities. He was eight years older than Joseph and much more a man of the world.

Aksyonov had helped Joseph in various ways after the trial, including trying to get him published so that he would have some sort of official status to protect him in the future. Their relations continued to be friendly in the West. Aksyonov was invited to America to teach in 1975, and he and Joseph did a series of readings together; on that trip they came to stay with us in Ann Arbor.

In 1980, after the *Metropol'* affair (which caused Carl and me to be banned from the USSR) and the

Italian publication of Aksyonov's most anti-Soviet work—*The Burn*—Aksyonov came to the United States again on a visit but was quickly stripped of his Soviet citizenship. In emigration Aksyonov and his wife would be as poor as everyone else—he needed to publish, and Carl thought he would have to teach, something he had never done before. Vasya Aksyonov came to Ann Arbor as we were publishing the Russian edition of *The Burn*. We were sure he would quickly find a publisher for the English.

Joseph was in New York at this time, and one day he was asked by someone at Farrar, Straus to read the manuscript of Akysonov's novel and give an evaluation. Joseph called Carl a few days after this and boasted that he had done a good job for them. (I was in Carl's study working, and I heard his end of this conversation.)

"I told them that the novel was shit," Joseph said proudly.

At this, Carl, who had for so long had been understanding of the poetic temperament, reached his limit: he told Joseph off. Joseph, angry and uncomprehending, asked what he should have done.

Carl told him he should have recused himself on the grounds that Aksyonov was his friend. Joseph broke into self-justification: Aksyonov was not really that close, the book was no good, et cetera.

Carl, with the list of second-raters Joseph had given blurbs to or helped get published fresh in his mind, refused to be nice about this.

"I am going to have to tell Vasya about this," Carl said. "You are destroying his career, and he doesn't know it—he thinks you are a friend."

Joseph appeared not to understand what he had done, how dishonorable it was, Carl told me.

"How convenient for him," was my reaction.

This was the danger point for our friendship with Joseph—he could easily turn against Carl for this, and that would be very sad after all we had been to each other. But Carl had no regrets.

Carl called Aksyonov the next day. Vasya was upset, but, as he told me later, he had been hearing rumors about Joseph's comments in New York but just didn't want to believe them. Much later still, Aksyonov told me that he finally called Joseph himself and had it out with him. He said something like this: Sit on your throne, decorating your poems with classical references, but leave the rest of us alone. You don't have to like us, but don't harm us, don't pretend to be our friend.

It would be four years before Aksyonov's novel was published in English by Random House.

I thought a great deal about this issue of the famous Soviet writers, because Joseph was so tone-deaf about it all. Normally he would catch himself being unkind and would remind himself to be charitable—but never with these people. Perhaps these stars became an embodiment of the Soviet Union for Joseph. The suspicion of being a sell-out extended even to people like Vladimir Vysotsky, the great singer-songwriter of the era.

It was something visceral and irrational, this hatred for the famous who had tried to help him. While it is understandable that Joseph would want to distance himself from those he considered compromised, it is harder to comprehend why he would turn to them for help. The most striking case of this ambivalence concerns the poet Evgeny Evtushenko.

Evtushenko, who was famous all over the world, had a freedom to travel that was unprecedented. This privilege aroused suspicions in many that he was a tool of the KGB, since everyone knew that the price of travel was to report back to that organization on everyone and everything you saw. Although no proof of Evtushenko's recruitment by the secret police has yet surfaced, he was working for them in the sense that a young, attractive poet embodied positive propaganda for the Soviet Union. Evtushenko was a "complex phenomenon," however, in that he had defended Sinyavsky and Daniel and had helped many other people. In America he managed to become friendly with the Kennedy family ... He was a Siberian and acted as if the rules didn't apply to him, as if his vast public was a form of protection. Joseph was hardly alone in being suspicious of him.

Evtushenko had made the mistake of boasting to Joseph that he had had something to do with Joseph's being allowed to emigrate: he said he had talked to someone high up, urging that Brodsky be treated decently as he was leaving. In Joseph's telling this at first changed into Evtushenko asking Premier Andropov to let Joseph go rather than arresting him.

A few years ago Evtushenko told his side of the story in a controversial and quite self-serving documentary on Russian television. It is three hours long, and one full hour is devoted to his relationship with Joseph Brodsky. Evtushenko said that he had merely taken the opportunity to ask a KGB acquaintance, not Andropov, that Joseph not be humiliated as he was on his way out of the country.

Later Joseph began to say that Evtushenko not only was working for the KGB, but that the older poet was actually the one responsible for sending him into exile. All of this was, of course, passed on to Evtushenko (they had many friends in common), who had things out with Joseph in person during one of his trips to the United States and thought that they had settled this "misunderstanding." However Joseph continued to say bad things about him to anyone who would listen, including to Evtushenko's ex-wife, Akhmadulina.

Despite all of this hostility, the next time Evtushenko was in New York Joseph went to see him at his hotel, wanting his help in getting his parents out, a story told by Joseph himself to the interviewer Solomon Volkov, who plays a tape of his interview with Joseph during the Evtushenko film. That Joseph would even seek out Evtushenko was amazing to me and speaks either to Joseph's despair or his lack of understanding of cause and effect. Joseph's parents could have emigrated (which

Joseph thought would be a disaster for them), but not even Henry Kissinger had been able to arrange a visit for them. Evtushenko promised Joseph help but apparently made the decision not to give it (something Evtushenko denied in his interview), which Joseph then found out.

Joseph got revenge later by writing a letter to Queens College about why they should not hire Evtushenko, the kind of letter featuring false statements that is always called a denunciation in Russia.

The Evtushenko feud did not end there: in May 1987 Joseph resigned from the American Academy and Institute of Arts and Letters in protest against the induction of Evtushenko as an honorary member. In his letter he accused the organization of fully compromising its integrity. This was widely seen as an act of petulance.

We agreed to disagree on many things with Joseph, a concept that was fairly alien to him. Once, after Carl's death, he asked me if Carl had ever been mad at him. I looked at him and saw that he really didn't understand the demands he had made of us, the promises he had not kept. I am sure we had disappointed him as well ...

"Sometimes," I answered, almost deafened by the sound of all that water flowing under the bridge.

Who were we for him? I am not sure—probably different things at different times. At first his New York world of literary celebrity made him see us as minor, I think, as people of the past, a category many of his Russian friends were destined to be assigned to. Later he began to see other values in us. Once he called and asked me what I thought of his play *Marbles*.

"Why do you ask me that?" I asked.

"Because you and Carl have common sense," he said.

Then I knew he wanted an honest reaction, probably in contrast to what he was getting in New York. We had published this play in Russian, but we had not given Joseph our opinion of it because he had not asked for it until then.

I was honest and told him it read like an unsuccessful mix of Stoppard and Beckett.

He said "OK, then."

Ardis had its own small fame in literary and publishing circles—we had been interviewed and profiled in newspapers almost from the beginning and Carl was often on the Voice of America. Before Joseph, however, we did not really know what fame was. Our policy about Joseph Brodsky was clear: fame could only help him and protect him, so we would do everything we could to aid this process. Usually Joseph had good instincts about how to handle such things, but at other times he would turn into the mulish prima donna he had been in Vienna until Strobe Talbott used psychology to keep him talking.

This is precisely what happened in 1981 when he met the producers from *60 Minutes*, who had come to Ann Arbor to see if Joseph Brodsky would be right for a segment on this very popular TV show. Everyone at Ardis was excited by the possibility of this famous program coming to our workspace in the basement.

Everyone, that is, but the poet himself. The producer doing the advance work was named Philip, as I recall, and after a long conversation with Joseph he came to me and said that he didn't think it would work.

"Why not?"

"Because Brodsky says he has no news value, he's just a Russian poet. That it wouldn't be interesting for anyone."

I saw that Philip was having doubts about the entire project because Joseph hadn't liked the questions and had turned sullen. I advised the producer to leave the subjects of prison and exile aside for the moment and ask Joseph about picking up girls with Baryshnikov in New York. This, of course, brought out Joseph's sense of humor and he became more approachable—and filmable.

In no time at all the famed interviewer Morley Safer was sitting in the Ardis packing room interviewing Joseph and us. Then the team went to New York to film, and that September the American audience heard Russian poetry in prime time. This program brought Joseph to the attention of people who normally had no interest in Russian literature, and the effects of such exposure are incalculable.

Joseph traveled in the summers, so I don't remember where he was when Carl was diagnosed with terminal colon cancer in the summer of 1982, but he came to visit him in his hospital room at NIH after a brutal first operation in September of that year. Joseph was stricken. He had been so sure that he would die first, not the seemingly healthy Carl.

In this year Joseph wrote the poem "Near Alexandria," dedicated to Carl. At first the title was "Washington," but then Joseph changed it, probably to underscore a connection with his beloved Cavafy, the poet of a very different Alexandria ... Although ostensibly a winter poem, July is mentioned because that was when Carl was diagnosed; the fallen colossus referred to in the poem is Carl himself.

I have a distinct memory of one moment after Carl's first operation, when Joseph stayed with us in Ann Arbor. He and I were alone, standing outside the house looking at the Huron River in the distance, and he told me that his first thought on hearing that Carl was sick had been that the KGB was somehow responsible. I could say nothing to that, but I did understand him. In his Sovietized psychology all evils led back to the system itself, and accidents—genetic or not—didn't happen.

A time of death was upon us in the 1980s, as the AIDS epidemic took Gena Smakov and many other friends. For Joseph the deaths of his mother in 1983 and his father in April 1984 were shattering, as can be seen in his essay about them.

In the spring of 1984 Carl, who had been through five operations and much experimental chemotherapy in two years, had enough strength to organize a forum on Russian culture in exile at the University of Michigan. Attending were Joseph, the writers Yuz

Aleshkovsky, Sasha Sokolov, Sergei Dovlatov, the painter David Miretsky, and Baryshnikov. After the forum, which had an unusually large audience thanks to Misha, we had a big party at our house. It would be Carl's last Russian-American party, and it was very enjoyable. Joseph, however, distinguished himself by being unpleasant to any Russians who were not old friends of his; his social phobia had not lessened with time and fame.

In September 1984 Carl died, and Joseph came for the wake along with a hundred other people close to Carl. He was warm and supportive, and I was very glad he was there.

I did not go to the memorial evening for Carl at the New York Public Library on April 1, 1985, but a number of people close to us took part, including Joseph, Arthur A. Cohen, Sasha Sokolov, and many others. Joseph gave a moving speech in which he acknowledged what Carl had done for him. The poet was hyperbolic in his praise of Ardis, but he was very accurate about Carl, and that mattered to me a great deal. "One sensed in his presence," he said, "that having taken the full measure of you, that he harbors no illusions about you—and yet he was kind." He discussed the value of a friend like Carl who could be—and was—called any time, day or night. I laughed when I read that part in the transcript a friend sent me: Joseph was thinking of a specific incident. Once in the early years Joseph had returned to Ann Arbor from Paris, and as far as we knew everything was normal. A few days later there was a frantic late-night call from Joseph begging Carl to drive a French girl to the airport, immediately. Joseph had to get rid of her, there was a flight, it was impossible to explain, but he would never ask anything like this again …

When I write about Joseph here, I see that I am also writing about Carl; I think of them together now, two men who were convinced they would not have long lives. As I write this, I consider for the first time the things Joseph and Carl Proffer had in common. They were both risk takers, literary men of action.

Joseph fought fear of death with poetry, love, sex, coffee, and cigarettes—and tried to deny death's significance while almost never being able to forget it. He knew his heart was bad (he had had his first heart attack in jail, right after his arrest), and we had all seen him clutch his chest in the middle of conversations, listen carefully to something only he could hear, and then resume the conversation, making some witty comment about the limitations of the body.

Carl's fear was seldom expressed. He told me early that he would not see fifty, but I rejected this as a kind of romanticism and was sure I had talked him out of it. These men were in a hurry, as if there might not be enough time to do what they had to do, and I was impatient by nature, so velocity was our natural element.

Joseph had many surrogate families, and probably they felt the same way as we did—charmed, intrigued, and certain they were enjoying a special intimacy. None of them, however, played the role Carl did in Joseph's life. There is a reason, beyond the fact of their deaths, that Joseph gave *Less Than One* this dedication: *In memory of my mother and my father/In memory of Carl Ray Proffer.*

Stockholm, 1987

One of Joseph's Leningrad friends claims that after the poet finished writing *Gorbunov and Gorchakov* in 1968, he said he'd get a Nobel for it someday. What rings true is Joseph's own belief in his work. This sort of confidence is a kind of genius in itself. All literary Russians were aware of the Nobel, especially since Pasternak had received it in 1958 and demonstrated that the award was in the realm of the possible for a Soviet writer.

The Nobel came up only once in our conversations that I remember: Joseph said to me that he and Milosz, who received the Nobel in 1980, nominated each other every year. Nonetheless, it was a big surprise to us all when Joseph actually got the prize. He called to tell me, but I had already heard—the news went around our world as fast as phone lines could carry it.

Joseph wanted me to come to the ceremony; I told him I didn't have the money, which was true; but I had other reasons—I was still in free fall from Carl's death.

I did not talk about this with Joseph, and only my closest friends in Ann Arbor knew how much trouble I was in. But Joseph insisted much more than he normally would have and sent me the money for the ticket (I paid him back later, which surprised him). And I went, somewhat unwillingly, to the Swedish capital in the dead of winter.

I was wrong to have resisted. I got to see Joseph as happy as I'd ever seen him: overwhelmed, confused, but, as always, up to the challenge. I was very glad he'd made me come. We met the afternoon before the ceremonies, and he was exhilarated and warm. He had an air and a smile that asked: can you believe that this has happened?

He had only so many tickets, so the group he invited as his guests was quite small (Venclova, Losev, old friends from New York). Also present were his American and European publishers and Russian friends who had found ways to get in as someone else's guest or as members of the press.

The event was very precisely managed, but it had some off-kilter aspects. When you gave your coat to the coat check for the banquet and ball, you were confronted by a black and white television showing hard-core porn, watched by the young man who took your coat ...

The acceptance speeches began; these speeches are a good deal more casual than the Nobel lectures and have the charm of something composed quickly. I remember how struck everyone was by the humility and grace of the Japanese biologist, Tonegawa.

Joseph took his place and began reading his speech in English very well, but about a third of the way through he switched to Russian intonation, and his English became very difficult to understand. The Swedes near me, all of whom spoke English fluently, asked what he was saying, and at times I couldn't tell either.

The ball began, and I saw some of the disheveled Soviet dissidents floating past as Tomas Venclova and I danced the first dance (partners were chosen for you, but we didn't know who did the choosing). Tomas and I were almost unable to make conversation, so odd and significant was this event.

Joseph himself was dancing with the queen of Sweden.

How had this happened? How had the little redhead from Leningrad, the boy who refused speech therapy for his Jewish accent, the teenager who had left school at fifteen, how had he gotten to this ceremony in Stockholm? We knew talent wasn't enough—Proust, Joyce, Borges, and Nabokov, for example, had been ignored by the Nobel Committee. As literary people we did believe in something called fate, which matched up with Joseph's own sense of destiny.

Many people had helped Joseph get to this place. Roger Straus, who did everything possible for Joseph in a professional sense, just as he did for Susan Sontag, deserves some credit. Roger, whom I personally disliked for the way he bullied those he considered unimportant, was remarkably astute about the business of building a literary reputation into something significant on the world stage, and Joseph owed him a great deal. The Polish poet Czeslaw Milosz was also important for Joseph's reputation, since his opinion was deeply respected in European circles. Milosz had come to Ann Arbor a number of times, where he had two publishers, Ardis and Michigan Slavic Materials. We had published his translations into English of Alexander Wat and a translation into Russian of one of Milosz's major works.

Joseph claimed that it was not interesting to talk to Milosz, no matter how much he liked him, because they agreed on everything. This was not true from what I saw. Milosz had been in the United States longer and was much less narrow in his ideas about poetry—he saw, as Joseph did not, the significance of Whitman, for example. He was thoughtful and considered about politics, quite different from his Russian friend.

Joseph's essays were important for the Nobel committee: they couldn't read the poems in Russian, but they could read the essays. The essays were uneven, but Joseph's intellect and powerful personality came through in every line.

When you know a writer personally, it is almost impossible to be a normal reader. When I reread Joseph's essays now, I am struck by both his insights and by his great, flattening generalizations, the focus on cause and effect, and the need to filter everything through the brain. The hectoring tone and ex cathedra pronouncements are not softened, as they were in life, by Joseph's sense of humor. He is brilliant when discussing poems by Auden and Tsvetaeva, but his expert analysis (which does not deal very much with sound itself), tends to explain most things by conscious choice, as if the unconscious played no role. Joseph is on record as saying that the unconscious hardly exists for a poet because he is so busy exploiting it. Naturally he projects his own qualities onto other poets. He is best when autobiographical, writing tenderly and gratefully about Auden and Spender as remarkable human beings whom he had the privilege of knowing.

If anyone wants to know what Joseph was like in a bad mood—having traveled by himself to a place where he did not know the language—one can read the dyspeptic, ill-considered essay on Istanbul, "Flight from Byzantium," in which he wades into waters too deep for him; or the essay on his trip to Brazil ("After a Journey") in the collection *On Grief and Reason*, in which he ends up referring to his Scandinavian girlfriend as "it."

In the essays on his own life, "Less Than One" and "In a Room and a Half," the language of logic and rationalization disappears: he has brought his best poetic self to his childhood and his beloved parents, and the result is sincerity raised to art.

The long essay about Venice, "Watermark," is a hybrid in that many of the lines are taken from his poetry. Here are the many sides of Joseph's character and talent, the joy in Venice (he says he felt like a cat, and there is no higher sign of happiness for him), the openness to its sensual appeal, sea sounds and water mixing together with incredible architecture. As soon as he turns his eyes to human beings, the tone changes; it seems to me that his irritation gets in the way of his intelligence as he attacks easily recognized Italian acquaintances for being leftists.

Brodsky the poet has for me considerably more varied qualities than Brodsky the essayist. I certainly considered Joseph Brodsky the greatest Russian poet since Pasternak, as did most of the Russian readers of the time. For those who could read him in the original, his range, his ambition, his determination to bring new subjects and new meters into Russian were signs of a major figure, one who made unusual demands on his Russian reader.

Memento mori is a key idea in Brodsky's work, and although it is an august poetic theme, for him it had a frightening reality. Exile, another common theme, seems to evoke a not entirely ironic self-pity as he places his subject, "a nobody in a raincoat," against the grandeur of European spaces, a man whose name "has been forgotten by entire cities," who has lost "his memory, his native land, and his son," and who says the century is ending—but that his end will come first. The poet's heaviness, his denial of consolation, can lie like fog over a scene, blocking out the light of creation. Only rarely does the poet address his maker and say that he is "grateful for it all." But the void is not necessarily negative, it can also be the pool from which possibilities arise. The subject may be dark, but the technical mastery on display cuts against it and can evoke exhilaration in the reader.

Even now all I have to do is open the first book we published, *Chast' rechi* (*A Part of Speech*), and read the "Twenty Sonnets to Mary Stuart" to feel that exhilaration, as the poet begins with the real Mary Stuart, switches to the movie star he fell in love with who played her, and finally rests on the girl, Marina, who reminded him of the movie star. Alternately playful and serious in these sonnets, the poet finds brilliant rhymes and makes difficult work look easy, like the cavalier with metaphysical interests that he was.

It is too early to say if Brodsky as a poet will be seen as the equal of Tsvetaeva and Mandelstam. I think the collections *Uraniia* (Urania), *Chast' rechi* (*A Part of Speech*), and *Novye stansy k Avguste* (*New Stanzas to Augusta*) are remarkable books of poetry. His prose is not on the level of Eliot's (and Eliot is very important to his development) or Mandelstam's, but it is an honor to Joseph that he can be considered in such company.

It is time, Joseph's subject and enemy, that determines a poet's place in his culture, of course, not my opinion, or even that of his first audience; but to be part of that first audience, as he came into maturity as a poet, was unforgettable, like witnessing the formation of a new galaxy.

A Birthday in New York: May 24, 1990

"There's going to be a big birthday party at my place," Joseph said on the phone. "You have to come, it's my fiftieth."

As the only child of an adoring mother, Joseph got very happy on his birthday. In Russia he had been used to an enormous crowd flooding in to his parents' large room—which they still did after he was gone. That May I walked into his apartment on Morton Street and saw all strata of his life represented: Russian, American, literary, medical …

Out back there was a tent and a raised dais sort of structure. As I arrived, Joseph and Derek Walcott were sitting on it, as if surveying their subjects. Joseph was warm in his welcome. I gave him a special present, his ornate candlestick from Leningrad, the one he had written a poem about, the one he had given us as a keepsake. I told him that I thought it should come back to him on this important birthday.

I knew many people at this party, but I did not feel relaxed. The Russian and American groups were not mixing well. I was glad to talk to Susan Sontag, who was lighting a cigarette as I came up. She was not supposed to be smoking and felt the need to explain: "I've turned having just one cigarette into a vice."

We talked a bit about Carl. When he was first diagnosed, Susan was one of the hundred people I called for advice and connections, and she was wonderful about it. This was not our chief subject on this day, however. What *was* on our minds at this birthday party was our complicated relationships with Joseph.

Susan and her son, David Rieff, who became Joseph's editor, were one of Joseph's families in New York. Then David Rieff wrote a negative review of Bloom's *The*

Closing of the American Mind, and Joseph broke off all relations with him. Since Joseph shared many if not all of Bloom's convictions (the literary canon is what matters) and prejudices, it is understandable that Joseph would disagree with Rieff's remark that Bloom was "vengeful and reactionary." It is less understandable to an American that Joseph would break a friendship over a book review. This again, was one of Joseph's blind spots: he was defending culture against the philistines, or, as he liked to call them, the "plebs."

Susan was bewildered by this side of Joseph. This was really a Soviet argument transposed to an American context. In Russia the stakes had been very high as an entire culture was first destroyed by the Bolsheviks and then by Stalin. So Joseph saw this review not just as an evaluation of Bloom's book but as an opening shot in what was possibly the long, slow destruction of culture in America. He placed no trust in the market of ideas because he had experienced the results of sudden, drastic political change that had led to loss of freedom.

As we were watching the procession of famous Russians and Americans going up to congratulate Joseph, I told Susan that Joseph could easily go off the rails: for example, he had threatened to sue me if I published Carl's memoirs of him. She was very surprised— she apparently thought that I was immune to his rage. She wanted to know what had happened and I gave her the short version, which was:

In 1984, the last year of Carl's life, as he lay on the chemo table (they were doing radical chemo at NIH, canting it directly into a hole in his abdomen to cause peritonitis), Carl was assembling his memoirs. Joseph was the last subject he got to before his death. He consulted our notes and diaries and incorporated everything he could, but he never got past a partial first draft of the section on Joseph. Carl made me promise to publish the memoirs even though some of them were essentially unfinished.

When it came time in early 1987 to make the memoirs into the book *The Widows of Russia*, I read the section on Joseph and came to the conclusion that I could not publish it without letting him see it first. He read it and was horrified, despite the fact that it conveyed our love and admiration for him. There were errors, he said, and I am sure there were—Carl had not begun the process of checking the things we had not personally witnessed. "I understand some of it is flattering," Joseph wrote, "but no, you can't publish this ..." He was upset by Carl's objectivity; a friend should not write this way. Joseph imagined that he could control what was written about him.

Carl was writing while in pain and facing death in the very near future, and that affected the tone of what he wrote. Nonetheless, in terms of how Joseph seemed to him and the degree of self-mythologizing he observed, for example, these notes truly reflected what Carl thought; whether he would have changed the tone of what he wrote in a later draft is an open question.

I was prepared to make cuts if Joseph insisted, but I was not prepared for Joseph's intense reaction: he felt betrayed, and he did not understand that I had made a promise to a dying husband. In a paranoid moment he blamed me, telling mutual friends that I must have written this, because Carl would never have done it. This was not very amusing at the time, especially when I was getting ready to print Joseph's next book in Russian.

When he sent me a letter threatening to sue me, I called my Russian *consigliere* Sarra Babyonysheva, who knew everyone in the Russian literary world. She in turn talked to Joseph's friend, Viktoria Schweitzer. Sarra then called me and said: take the Brodsky section out of Carl's book, you'll publish it later. It's not worth it to destroy such a close friendship.

I agreed to this, but I added a line to my preface saying that the Brodsky memoir had been taken out at the request of the author.

Susan absorbed all of this sadly; she had liked Carl. She asked me how the friendship had recovered from this terrible threat.

"I had to make the decision to forgive Joseph," I said. Now I think it would have been truer to say that I couldn't bear to lose another person from my life.

She clearly had trouble with the idea of just forgiving him for such a threat. I don't think she had yet forgiven Joseph for David or for what had happened between them. Yet she was there, at that party, as was I. Later Joseph and David Rieff would make up ...

And this is a marker of something in Joseph's personality. He could break your heart, he could outrage your sense of honor and justice, but you would forgive him in the name of something hard to name. He himself was so vulnerable, so childlike in certain ways. Even in his rages he was capable of catching himself, and then he would try to reverse the damage done to his concept of himself as a decent person. This process was usually transparent and utterly disarming. But not always.

The Nobel had disoriented Joseph: he had won, and now he had money. This so little suited his self-concept that he got rid of the money as fast as he could. Sometimes he would complain bitterly to me about the bad things someone was saying about him, and I would remind him that none of it mattered—he had won the Nobel, and, really, every other prize worth having as well. He needed his enemies; resisting them—and the state—had formed his identity.

After I talked to a few of my Russian friends at this party—Yuz Aleshkovsky and his wife, Lena and Sergei Dovlatov, I went to say goodbye to Joseph. He walked me out and then stopped.

"We have come a long way," he said, with quiet tenderness in the middle of this large party.

"Yes," I said, thinking that he meant—a long way to this moment.

Later I realized that I had perhaps misunderstood—he had started using "we" meaning "you," and maybe he just meant that I had come all the way from Michigan for this party. I would only know what he really meant later, when I read his last note to me.

The party took place in May. By September Joseph's life had utterly changed.

He acted befuddled when he told me about it.

"I can't believe it, I don't know what I did," he said.

I asked him what had happened.

"I got married … It's just … it's just the girl is so beautiful."

The implication was that, against his better judgment, her beauty had forced him to marry her. Given his previous history, I was very surprised.

"You've been with lots of beautiful women, but you didn't marry them," I said. "There's more to it than her beauty. "

"I don't know," he said.

I remember hanging up, struck that this had happened so late in his life. My mind immediately went to two crucial events of the previous year, 1989, events that in my view made it possible for Joseph to marry.

The crumbling of the Soviet Union in 1989 astounded all of us. There were really only two people I knew who had predicted change of any sort: Andrei Amalrik and Stephen F. Cohen. The rest of us thought it would be another thirty years before the Soviet monolith crumbled. Like many émigrés, Joseph was afraid to believe events were really as reported. Even when I came back from the Moscow Book Fair that year and told him that everything had changed, he was still suspicious. This is a trick, he said, and many people agreed with him. Expecting the worst was an intelligent position when discussing the Soviet Union.

In these years, like all of his friends, I was very worried about Joseph's physical condition. His formidable resilience was showing signs of fraying around the edges. He met me at JFK Airport on my way back from Russia, and apropos of nothing he reported: "women still treat me like a lay." Oh, you have learned English, was my first thought. And then I realized that he was reporting that the heart medicines he took had not yet affected his sex life. His many heart operations, which included two heart bypasses, had required every bit of his strength and resilience, and after each recovery came the fear that he would not be able to write poetry.

The year 1989 brought Joseph an important visitor: the twenty-two-year-old Andrei Basmanov, the son who had last seen his father when he was five. Things did not go well. Joseph called me up and said with disgust that his son, who played the guitar, did nothing all day but watch MTV, saying that they had nothing like this in Russia.

Of course, he likes it. He's a young musician, I said. I like it myself.

He doesn't read. He knows nothing, said Joseph angrily.

This was the real crime. His son was supposed to be a copy of him and make him proud. I told him to take it easy on the kid, who was meeting his father as an adult for the first time. He could not do it, he was too disappointed. The next time we talked about it, Andrei had gone back to Russia ahead of time. Joseph was still upset and blamed Marina for how Andrei had turned out. No longer would he be against having another child who might make Andrei feel displaced, as he had once told me.

This visit connected to the second major event of this year. Joseph found out that Marina had gotten married, and he wrote a final, very bitter poem to her in which he actually found a rhyme for chemical engineer. In a sense, he had remained married to Marina until that moment.

I went to London for a meeting of the jury for the Russian Booker Prize, and it was then that I met Maria Sozzani Brodsky, at Diana Myers's house. Now I got a look at the more that there was to it. She was not only remarkably beautiful, much more than even the photographs show, she was intelligent and cultured. Descended from Italians and aristocratic Russians, she spoke four languages, was a classical pianist, and her main interest as a student of Russian literature was Tsvetaeva. Although she had never been to Russia, she was of his world: she had been very close to the Etkind family in emigration, a Leningrad family Joseph had known well. All that and beauty—how could he not have married her?

Maria was much younger than he, and in London, when we were walking out to say goodbye (naturally the important things were always said then), he brought up her youth as a concern. I told him that if she wanted children, he should agree to it. With Carl's death I saw the equations of marriage and children in a different light—I was very grateful that we'd had our daughter Arabella in 1978. I did not think, at that point, that Joseph had very long to live, and I assumed that Maria understood the fragility of his health. But at this moment he looked happy and well. He seemed to have gotten used to the idea that he was married.

By 1993 he had a daughter, Anna, nicknamed Niushka, and was living in Brooklyn with his new family. Maria would give him the thing he had not ever really had, a domestic life.

In 1995 Joseph asked me to publish his new book of poetry, *Peizazh s navodneniem (Landscape with Flood)*, in Russian. By this time I had moved to California with my daughter, Arabella Proffer, and my husband, Ross Teasley, and I was rarely in New York. I had assumed that Joseph would do his next book with a publishing house in Russia, but he had once again turned against Russia: he said his books published there were ugly, badly done, vulgar, and so on. I sensed that wasn't the key reason: he was making some sort of point by this decision.

Even though I knew a Russian publisher would end up doing the book after me, I agreed because he had done all of his major books with us first; although it made no sense for Ardis financially, he was our author.

In January 1996 I came to New York, and on January 18 I went with Mary Ann Szporluk and Ron Meyer, two Ardis editors well known to Joseph, to the new Brodsky family apartment in Brooklyn.

Joseph had been forced to move from his cozy Village apartment soon after he broke the first rule of New York housing: he had completely remodeled a rental apartment. Soon after the owner turned it into a condo, one that was too small for Joseph and his new wife. This was but one of Joseph's many successful efforts to get rid of the Nobel money. He was impractical by nature, but he was also guilt-prone and quite aware that Beckett, a model of artistic austerity, had given away all of his Nobel money.

The Brooklyn apartment was very nice, very comfortable. Maria was charming to us. Little Niushka, who looked very like a Brodsky, was about two years old and already talking fluently. Maria read poetry to her and was obviously doing everything to encourage her development. I talked a little to her, but my mind was on how bad Joseph looked. He was putting off yet another operation ...

He had always been able to summon a stoical sort of cheerfulness ("Life is shit," he said, comforting our friend Nancy Beardsley once, "but that's no reason not to have fun"), and even now he pursued different projects with energy, meeting friends and staying in the game, but anyone talking to him could feel him watching time running out.

We were very happy to see each other. Joseph and I fell into our normal conversational mode. He told me his health was getting worse, and I said, well, you've been living on borrowed time for so long. This was a normal exchange for Joseph and me, but I think it was hard on Maria, and I was sorry for that frankness when I looked at her face.

Joseph showed me his study, which had its own door to the street, and I saw that he had made another nest like his room in Leningrad—much bigger, much more nicely furnished—but identical in atmosphere. He gave me a child's poem to read, one written in English. He was excited, his pleasure in writing was still there.

I don't remember whether he said this about Maria that day or on the phone after, but to my comment that she seemed like a good person, he said: "She's pure inside and out." And that's when I knew that he felt she was too good for him.

After New York I went on to Washington, DC, where I met one of my Moscow friends, Zhenia Gavrilova.

"How is Joseph?" she asked.

"His face is the color of ashes," I said without thinking.

Despite this, I did not think he was dying. He had been in this condition before and had survived. I went home and worked on his book. On January 23, 1996, I received a handwritten fax from him asking if a new poem could be added at the last minute. Then he added a paragraph in English about my visit: "Watching you chatting with Anna was truly overwhelming for me: it felt like coming full circle. From carrying Ian on my shoulders through our corridor in Leningrad to you talking to Niushka (in English), quite a distance seems to have been covered by both of us. Send me a picture of Arabella. Kisses, Joseph."

Five days later, on January 28, he died in his study. Despite everything I knew about his health, I was surprised. It seemed impossible that I would never hear his voice again.

I happened to talk to Vasya Aksyonov a few days later.

It feels like the end of an era, I said. This cliché had never felt so new.

Yes, said Vasya, it does. Like almost everyone else, Vasya had forgiven Joseph everything.

I would go to the memorial evening for Joseph and the reception afterwards, but this moment on the phone was when I truly knew that he was gone, and it left me breathless.

The Akhmatova Museum, 2003

I encountered the problems of the afterlife of fame when I made a trip to the native city of both Joseph Brodsky and Vladimir Nabokov in 2003, and literary themes came together in ways that would have satisfied the author of *The Gift*. We are all familiar with the habit of imposing meaning on events, of seeing connections that may or may not exist. Less familiar is what I experienced now, a kind of refusal to see connections that are evident even as you perceive events as separate and sealed off from each other.

I was going to St. Petersburg because of Joseph for the first time since he left Russia. Officially I was there to represent the United States at an exhibit called "Joseph Brodsky: Urania. Leningrad—Venice—New York." The first such exhibit in Russia featured a collection of books, manuscripts, photographs, and memorabilia.

The city was newly gilded for its tercentenary—it had never in my lifetime been so clean or so beautiful. When you study Russian literature at first it will be Pushkin's city, then Dostoevsky's, but after a while you form your own literary associations with this artificial beauty erected over a swamp by Peter the Great.

I associated this unreal city not just with Joseph but also with the poets who had distilled its essence in many poems. "We will gather again in Petersburg, as if we've buried the sun there," wrote Mandelstam, and I kept thinking of him and his friend Akhmatova as my husband Ross and I walked around the city. The Russophile in me wished that Joseph had been buried in this city, where his origins and his readers were; but as someone who knew him well, I can say that I am sure he is happy to be buried on the island of San Michele in the Venetian Lagoon, in the company of Diaghilev and Stravinsky.

I was not prepared for the emotional aspects of the opening of the Brodsky exhibit, which was held at the Akhmatova Museum, located in the beautiful Fountain House, where she had a room for many years. I had never been in this famous building. Everything in the museum was familiar to me, although I was seeing it for the first time: the photographs of Akhmatova in the entrance area were ones Ardis had published thirty years earlier.

We had published many translations of Akhmatova, as well as reprints in Russian of some of her beautiful little books from the 1910s—and not just because we knew her friend, Nadezhda Mandelstam. Akhmatova's literary personality and fate were compelling, and both Carl and I had naturally been drawn to her. He translated her *Poem without a Hero*, and I had collected many of her photographs.

The director of the museum, Nina Popova, gave me a book as a present; she could hardly have guessed how interested I would be in this fascinating study of Akhmatova and the Fountain House.

Already a little off-balance, I walked through a doorway and saw TV monitors scattered on the floor, a Joseph on every screen. Our Ardis editions were part of this show, as was an entire wall of postcards Joseph had sent to his parents from his travels. His study at South Hadley was to some degree reassembled—typewriter, photos, desk objects, and so on.

I passed through another door and saw people I had not seen for decades: Joseph's friends. The sense of the past returned was powerful.

Friends told me about the plans for a Brodsky museum to be located in his family's old room. Tanya Nikolskaya came up to tell me that at that very moment a sculpture contest was taking place in the city, to choose the best bust or statue of Joseph.

"You'll like this," Tanya said. "Some of the statues are based on photos of him. One of them is Joseph stepping off a curb; another is him sitting on his suitcase at the airport ..."

Mr. *Mauvais Ton* would have laughed—and then have cried.

Several people spoke at the opening ceremony, which was covered by the media: the American ambassador, Alexander Vershbow; the representative of Alfa Bank, which partially underwrote the event; and I. All I remember of my improvised talk is that I began with a story, oddly, but appropriately, about Mandelstam.

In 1998 I had interviewed Emma Gerstein, the one person of the Mandelstam-Akhmatova circle who had a long life. My daughter Arabella would film the interview—yet another sign of how much Russia had changed: Emma would have been terrified of a foreigner with a camera in the old days.

Emma Gerstein had been part of my Russian life since 1970, but I could never really like her because she would begin every visit with an attack on her nemesis, Nadezhda Mandelstam; ultimately Carl, who was much more patient, went to see her without me. Emma lived a very long life, writing and writing until she seemed to merge with her desk; finally in great old age her memoirs made her famous in the newly free Russia.

Emma had prepared answers to everything, so I decided to ask something different in an attempt to evoke spontaneity.

"What were Osip Mandelstam's gestures like?"

At first she was nonplussed, and then she said: "When he shook my hand for the first time, I felt electricity."

And this is how meeting Joseph Brodsky was, I said to the audience at the Akhmatova Museum— electrifying.

I listened to many talks during these days and was disturbed to hear Joseph consistently portrayed as a martyr, even by those who knew him. Maybe that's how they saw him, or maybe that's what they thought would be good for his posthumous career in Russia. I could not fathom it. He would have found this unbearable.

Partly in reaction to this new party line, I spoke in a very different vein at the US consulate in front of a mostly Russian audience the night of the exhibit. I began by saying that I had never known anyone who wanted to leave the Soviet Union more than Joseph did. When he did leave, I told them, he lost something of vital importance: his audience. But you lost something important as well, I said—you lost your poet, and that is a terrible thing; perhaps this exhibit, with his books, desk, and photographs, is in a way an answer to fate.

One of his friends challenged me. Perhaps he wanted to go, he said, but certainly Joseph wanted to be able to come back.

Did he? I asked. I was one of the many who tried to convince him to visit Russia after 1989.

Joseph had many stated reasons for not going back. He said different things, depending on his time and mood, so all one can really trust are his actions. He did not return to his native country when he could have. I know a few of his reasons: one was the iron conviction that return would be a form of forgiveness. He could not believe the new masters were really that different from the old masters, the ones who had refused to let his parents out. Exile was so difficult that it was hard to believe one could just go back as if it had not cost you anything. As Americans descended from immigrants, we are familiar with this phenomenon: sometimes you love your country but it doesn't love you back. This loss becomes a part of your new identity.

This is the poet who wrote of staying in Russia: "There I'll die of boredom or fear ..." If going into exile is a way to change your fate, what would a return signify?

Themes of Brodsky and Nabokov wove together in Petersburg, sometimes comically. The day after the consulate reception Olga Voronina, one of the young women connected with the Nabokov Museum, took me to a radio station for an interview to publicize my lecture on Nabokov that evening at the museum.

The radio station was dingily familiar: it had an ancient, stained couch, undrinkable coffee, and personable people. The host, Natasha, was starting a sort of literary hour, and it began with an audience quiz, the prize being an art album. The audience was given the following hints: "Who left school at fifteen and went on to win the Nobel Prize?"

We did the interview about Nabokov, and then came time for the questions from the listeners. Joseph, who had not been the subject, was very much on their minds, since my friendship with him had been mentioned ...

"Is it true that Nabokov bought Brodsky jeans?" asked the first caller, determined to separate fact from fiction.

"No," I said. "Nabokov sent us money, and we bought the jeans."

The next caller was hostile; he wanted to know if it was true that Brodsky got the Nobel because he had his connections arrange it for him.

"Well," I said, "many people have connections, but not everyone gets the Nobel Prize."

That evening I went to speak at the Nabokov Museum, located in the Nabokov family's former apartment on Morskaya. I had never been there either. With *Speak, Memory* fresh in my mind, it was odd to be walking through Nabokov's emotional real estate. At that time the museum was struggling for funds and things were a bit shabby, but the rooms were beautiful. It was a very different space from Akhmatova's small room in Fountain House and Joseph's cubby in the Muruzi House. What all these places had in common, however, was their central location—they were good addresses under both Russian and Soviet skies.

As I was speaking about my impressions of the Nabokovs, I noticed that one man was half-turned away from me in what appeared to be mute fury. When question time came, he pronounced a tirade against Nabokov because the writer had made fun of the nineteenth-century writer Chernyshevsky in *The Gift*. This man seemed a thoroughly Dostoevskian character, and I understood that he was offended by Nabokov's elitism, his seeming lack of compassion for ordinary people.

"Well," I said, "one can hardly expect Nabokov to like someone like Chernyshevsky who supposedly said that boots matter more than culture."

At this the underground man stalked out. Nabokov himself would have understood: this man was waiting for someone to love Chernyshevsky as much as he did. And Joseph, who admired Dostoevsky, would have understood someone who took a literary grudge so seriously.

Joseph came up again that evening, and I began to think that he had actually known everyone in Leningrad; or perhaps it was that everyone had known him. The eminent cardiologist, Yasha Bagrov, a friend of our good friends in California, Lena and Igor Dzyaloshinsky, had come to the lecture and was taking us to his apartment on the Vyborg Side section of the city. The drive in the gypsy cab should have taken twenty minutes, but we hit a mystery traffic jam that lasted for two hours, during which we had a free-floating Russian conversation, the kind we could not have had under Soviet power, when you never knew who the driver was reporting to.

Yasha, half-blind and wholly discerning, had known Joseph, who had consulted him several times about his heart condition just before he left the country. He remembered that Joseph had been incredibly excited at the idea of going.

And yet some of his friends here want to see him as a victim, tragically forced into exile, I said.

Some of those friends are more like *official government* people than literary people, Yasha said. (The word is *gosudarstvennyi* in Russian, and it is often used sardonically.) It began to occur to me that Joseph could actually be used as part of the enormous patriotism project underway. This word and its implications stuck in my mind, and perhaps it was this offhand comment that led me to write these memoirs years later.

When we got to Yasha's apartment building, it was dark and he warned us to look around carefully before getting out of the car. He paid the driver to stay to drive us back. Safer that way, he said.

Putin's cleanup campaign had not reached this area of the city, which had once been middle-class. The building was in bad shape, the staircase had no railings, and the darkness was full of threat.

Inside the apartment, however, was all the warmth and charm of the Russian family. I recognized a constant feature of my entire Russian life: one passed through a door from the forbidding, unpromising outside into the vital intimacy within, from the coldly official to the warmly personal.

When it was time for us to go, Yasha flashed a light to our gypsy cab and made sure there were no lurkers in the parking area. It reminded me of Moscow in 1991, when old ladies were selling the family silver to feed their cats and I looked down an empty street and saw nothing unusual yet sensed great danger. This was a post-Soviet world neither Nabokov nor Brodsky had known.

I liked the Nabokov Museum and the Akhmatova Museum; I was glad there were such things in memory of these great writers. So why was I so upset at the idea of a Brodsky Museum? Later it came to me that you can resume grieving and not know it until something shocks you into awareness—like your hatred of the idea of a museum for a friend.

There is a Brodsky stamp in America, and there is an Aeroflot plane with his name on it. I don't want there to be a museum for Joseph, I don't want to see him on a stamp, or his name on the side of a plane—these things mean he is dead dead dead dead, and no one was ever more alive.

I protest: a magnetic and difficult man of flesh is in the process of being devoured by a monument, a monstrous development considering just how human Joseph was.

Joseph Brodsky was the best of men and the worst of men. He was no monument to justice or tolerance.

He could be so lovable that you would miss him after a day; he could be so arrogant and offensive that you would wish the sewers would open up under his feet and suck him down. He was a personality.

The poet's destiny was to rise, like his autumn hawk, into that upper atmosphere even if it was going to cost him everything. The only god he served was the god of poetry, and of that god he was a faithful servant. What made him believe in a higher power was the fact of his miraculous gift itself. And, like Blok, he was a poet every minute of every day.

Joseph Brodsky was full of fire and prejudice, a thirst for recognition, and genius. This, it turns out, is how I like my poets.

2014

ARDIS TITLES 1971–2002

English Language and Bilingual Books

ABRAMOV, Fyodor. Two Winters and Three Summers (1984)

AKHMATOVA, Anna. My Half Century: Selected Prose (1992)

AKHMATOVA, Anna. A Poem without a Hero (1973)

AKHMATOVA, Anna. Selected Poems (1976)

AKSYONOV, Vassily. The Destruction of Pompeii and Other Stories (1991)

AKSYONOV, Vassily. Our Golden Ironburg (1989)

AKSYONOV, Vassily. The Steel Bird and Other Stories (1979)

AKSYONOV, Vassily. Surplussed Barrelware (1985)

ANDREYEVA, Olga Chernov. Cold Spring in Russia (1978)

ANNENSKY, Innokenty. The Cypress Chest/Kiparisovyi larets (bilingual) (1982)

ANTONYCH, Bohdan. Square of Angels: Selected Poems (1977)

ARNDT, Walter, ed. Pushkin Threefold: Narrative, Lyric, Polemic, and Ribald Verse (first Ardis ed., 1993)

BABEL, Isaak. The Forgotten Prose (1978)

BAKHTIN, Mikhail. Problems of Dostoevsky's Poetics (1973)

BAKUNIN, Mikhail. From out of the Dustbin (1984)

BARABTARLO, Gennadi. Phantom of Fact: A Guide to
Nabokov's *Pnin* (1989)

BELKNAP, Robert L., ed. Russianness: In Memory of
Rufus W. Mathewson (1990)

BELOZERSKAYA, Lyubov. My Life with Mikhail
Bulgakov (1983)

BELY, Andrei. Complete Short Stories (1979)

BELY, Andrei. Kotik Letaev (1971)

BIALOSZEWSKI, Miron. A Memoir of the Warsaw
Uprising (1977)

BIRGER, Boris. Catalogue (1975)

BITOV, Andrei. Life in Windy Weather (1986)

BITOV, Andrei. Pushkin House (1990)

BITSILLI, Peter. Chekov's Art (1983)

BOYD, Brian. Nabokov's *Ada:* The Place of Consciousness
(1985)

BRODSKY, Joseph. A Stop in the Desert (broadside)
(1973)

BROWN, Edward J. *Brave New World, 1984*, and *We*: An
Essay on Anti-Utopia (1976)

BROWN, Nathalie Babel. Hugo and Dostoevsky (1978)

BROWN, William Edward. A History of 18th-Century
Russian Literature (1980)

BROWN, William Edward. A History of Russian
Literature of the Romantic Period, 4 vols. (1986)

BROWN, William Edward. A History of 17th-Century
Russian Literature (1980)

BROWNING, Gary. Boris Pilniak (1985)

BULGAKOV, Mikhail. Diaboliad and Other Stories
[second edition] (1992)

BULGAKOV, Mikhail. The Master and Margarita
(1995)

BULGAKOV, Mikhail. Notes on the Cuff and Other Stories (1991)

CATTAFI, Bartolo. The Dry Air of Fire and Other Poems (1982)

CERNY, Vaclav. Dostoevsky and His "Devils" (1975)

CHAPPLE, R. A Dostoevsky Dictionary (1982)

CHARENTS, Eghishe. Land of Fire: Selected Poems (1986)

CHERNYSHEVSKY, Nikolai. What Is to Be Done? (1988)

CHUDAKOV, A, P. Chekhov's Poetics (1983)

CHUKOVSKY, Kornei. Alexander Blok as Man and Poet (1982)

CHUKOVSKY, Kornei. Poet and Hangman (Nekrasov and Muravyov) (1977)

CIORAN, Samuel D. The General's Daughter (bilingual) (1993)

CIORAN, Samuel D. Russian Alive! (bilingual) (1992)

CIORAN, Samuel D. Welcome to Divnograd (bilingual) (1992)

COHEN, Arthur A. Osip Emilievich Mandelstam: An Essay in Antiphon (1974)

CONANT, Roger. The Political Poetry and Ideology of F. I. Tiutchev (1983)

DAVIES, Jessie. Esenin: A Biography in Memoirs, Letters, and Essays (1982)

De QUILLE, Dan. Dives and Lazarus (1988)

DOSTOEVSKY, Fyodor. The Complete Letters, 5 vols. (1988-91)

DOSTOEVSKY, Fyodor. The Crocodile: An Extraordinary Event, or a Show in the Arcade (1985)

DOSTOEVSKY, Fyodor. The Double: Two Versions (1985)

DOSTOEVSKY, Fyodor. Poor Folk (1983)

DOSTOEVSKY, Fyodor. The Unpublished Dostoevsky: Diaries and Notebooks (1860–81), 3 vols. (1973–76)

DOVLATOV, Sergei. Inostranka: A Russian Reader (bilingual) (1995)

DOVLATOV, Sergei. The Invisible Book (1979)

DUROVA, Nadezhda. The Cavalry Maid: The Memoirs of a Woman Soldier of 1812 (1988)

EIKHENBAUM, Boris. Lermontov (1981)

EIKHENBAUM, Boris. Russian Prose (1985)

EIKHENBAUM, Boris. Tolstoi in the Sixties (1982)

EIKHENBAUM, Boris. Tolstoi in the Seventies (1982)

EIKHENBAUM, Boris. The Young Tolstoi (1972)

ERDMAN, Nikolai. "The Mandate" and "The Suicide" (1975)

EVREINOV, Nikolai. Life as Theater: Five Modern Plays by Nikolai Evreinov (1973)

FETZER, Leland, ed. Pre-Revolutionary Russian Science Fiction (1982)

FIENE, Donald. Alexander Solzhenitsyn: An International Bibliography (1973)

FISHER, Lynn, and FISHER, Wesley. The Moscow Gourmet: Dining Out in the Capital of the USSR. A Guide (1974)

FLORIDI, Alexis U. Moscow and the Vatican (1986)

FODOR, Alexander. Tolstoy and the Russians: Reflections on a Relationship (1984)

FONVIZIN, Denis. Political Writings (1985) [Is this the correct title: The Political and Legal Writings of Denis Fonvizin?—DM]

FOWLER, Douglas. A Reader's Guide to *Gravity's Rainbow* (1980)

FRANTZ, Phillip. Gogol: A Bibliography (1989)

FYODOROV, Vadim. An Ordinary Magic Watch (1977)

GALICH, Alexander. Songs and Poems (1983)

GAZDANOV, Gaito. An Evening with Claire (1988)

GEORGE, Emery. The Boy and the Monarch (1987)

GEORGE, Emery. Kate's Death (1980)

GEORGE, Emery. Voiceprints (1987)

GEORGE, Emery, ed. Contemporary East European Poetry (1983)

GIPPIUS, Vassily. Gogol (1981)

GLADILIN, Anatoly. The Making and Unmaking of a Soviet Writer (1979)

GLADILIN, Anatoly. Moscow Racetrack (1990)

GOGOL, Nikolai. Arabesques (1982)

GOGOL, Nikolai. Hanz Kuechelgarten (1990)

GOLOVSKOY, Valery, and RIMBERG, John. Behind the Soviet Screen: The Motion-Picture Industry in the USSR, 1972–1982 (1986)

GONCHAROV, Ivan. An Ordinary Story (1994)

GONCHAROV, Ivan. The Precipice (1994)

GOSCILO, Helena. Lives in Transit: A Collection of Recent Russian Women's Writing (1995)

GOSCILO, Helena, and Lindsey, Byron. Glasnost: An Anthology of Russian Literature under Gorbachev (1990)

GOSCILO, Helena, and Lindsey, Byron. The Wild Beach and Other Stories (1992)

GREEN, Michael. The Russian Symbolist Theatre (1986)

GREEN, Michael, and Katsell, Jerome. The Unknown Russian Theater (1991)

KOCHINA, Elena. Blockade Diary (1990)

KOSTELANETZ, Richard. Portraits from Memory (1976)

KUZMIN, Mikhail. Wings: Prose and Poetry (1972)

LAURIDSEN, Inger Thorup, and DALGAARD, Per. The Beat Generation and the Russian New Wave (1990)

LAWTON, Anna. Vadim Shershenevich: From Futurism to Imaginism (1981)

LAZARD, Naomi. Ordinances (1978)

LEATHERBARROW, William, and OFFORD, Derek, eds. Documentary History of Russian Thought (1987)

LEHRMAN, Edgar. A Guide to the Russian Texts of Tolstoi's *War and Peace* (1980)

LEITER, Sharon. The Lady and the Bailiff of Time (1974)

LERMONTOV, Mikhail. Hero of Our Time (first Ardis ed., 1988)

LERMONTOV, Mikhail. Vadim (1984)

LEZHNEV, Abram. Pushkin's Prose (1983)

LOTMAN, Yury. Analysis of the Poetic Text (1976)

LOWE, David. Turgenev's *Fathers and Sons* (1983)

LUCKYJ, George. Before the Storm: Soviet Ukrainian Fiction of the 1920s (1986)

LUKER, Nicholas, ed. An Anthology of Russian Neo-Realism. The "Znanie" School of Maxim Gorky (1982)

LUKER, Nicholas, ed. From Furmanov to Sholokhov: An Anthology of the Classics of Socialist Realism (1988)

LUPLOW, Carol. Babel's *Red Cavalry* (1982)

LVOV-ROGACHEVSKY, V. A History of Russian-Jewish Literature (1979)

McKAIN, David. In Touch (1975)

McVAY, Gordon. Esenin: A Life (1976)

McVAY, Gordon. Isadora and Esenin (1979)

MAK, Lev. From the Night and Other Poems (1978)

MAKANIN, Vladimir. "Escape Hatch" and "The Long Road Ahead": Two Novellas (1996).

MANDELSTAM, Nadezhda. Mozart and Salieri: An Essay on Osip Mandelstam and Poetic Creativity (1973)

MANDELSTAM, Osip. Complete Critical Prose and Letters (1979)

MASON, Bobbie Ann. Nabokov's Garden: A Guide to *Ada* (1974)

MATICH, Olga, and HEIM, M., eds. The Third Wave: Russian Literature in Emigration (1983)

MENDELSON, Danuta. Metaphor in Babel's Short Stories (1982)

MERRILL, Reed, and FRAZIER, Thomas. Arthur Koestler: An International Bibliography (1979)

MERSEREAU, John. Orest Somov (1989)

MERSEREAU, John. Russian Romantic Fiction (1983)

MEYER, Priscilla, and RUDY, Stephen, eds. Dostoevsky and Gogol: Texts and Criticism (1979)

MIKHAILOVSKY, Nikolai. Dostoevsky: A Cruel Talent (1978)

MILLER, Frank. A Handbook of Russian Verbs (bilingual) (1988)

MILLER, Tamara. Bibliographical Index to *Novyi Mir* (1983)

MILOSLAVSKY, Yury. Urban Romances (1994)

MOCHULSKY, Konstantin. Andrei Bely (1976)

MOODY, Fred. Ten Bibliographies of Russian Literature (1977)

MORRISON, R. H., ed. America's Russian Poets (1975)

NABOKOV, Vladimir, trans. The Song of Igor's Campaign (1988)

NAGIBIN, Yury. The Peak of Success and Other Stories (1986)

NAKHIMOVSKY, A. D., and PAPERNO, V. A. A Russian-English Dictionary of Nabokov's *Lolita* (1982)

NAPPELBAUM, Moisei. Our Age/Nash Vek (bilingual) (1983)

NARBIKOVA, Valeria. *Day Equals Night*, 1999

NARBIKOVA, Valeria. *In the Here and There*, 1999

NEWLIN, Margaret. The Book of Mourning (1982)

NEWLIN, Margaret. Collected Poems (1986)

NEWLIN, Margaret. The Snow Falls Upward: Poems 1963–1975 (1976)

O'BELL, Leslie. Pushkin's "Egyptian Nights" (1984)

O'CONNOR, Katherine. Boris Pasternak's "My Sister-Life": The Illusion of Narrative (1989)

OKUDZHAVA, Bulat. 65 Songs/65 pesen (bilingual) (1980)

OKUDZHAVA, Bulat. Songs. Volume II (bilingual) (1986)

OKUDZHAVA, Bulat. A Taste of Liberty (1986)

OLESHA, Yury. The Complete Plays (1983)

OLESHA, Yury. The Complete Short Stories and "The Three Fat Men" (1979)

OLESHA, Yury. Envy (1975)

OLESHA, Yury. No Day without a Line (1979)

OSORGIN, Mikhail A. Selected Stories, Reminiscences, and Essays (1982)

OSTROVSKY, Alexander. The Storm (1988)

OSTROVSKY, Alexander. Without a Dowry and Other Plays (1996)

PASSAGE, Charles. Character Names in Dostoevsky (1982)

PASTERNAK, Boris. My Sister Life (1982)

PATERA, Tatiana. A Concordance to the Poetry of Anna
   Akhmatova (1995)

PAVLOVA, Karolina. A Double Life (1978)

PETERSEN, Carl. Each in Its Ordered Place: A Faulkner
   Collector's Notebook (1975)

PETERSON, Ronald. The Russian Symbolists (1986)

PILNYAK, Boris. Mahogany and Other Stories (1993)

PILNYAK, Boris. The Naked Year (1975)

PISEMSKY, Alexei. "Nina," "The Comic Actor," and "An
   Old Man's Sin" (1988)

PLATONOV, Andrei. Chevengur (1978)

PLATONOV, Andrei. Collected Works (1978)

PLATONOV, Andrei. The Foundation Pit/Kotlovan
   (bilingual) (1973)

POGORELSKY, Antony. The Double or My Evenings in
   Little Russia (1988)

POWERS, D. B. Dictionary of Russian Verb Forms (1985)

PROFFER, Carl. A Book of Things about Vladimir
   Nabokov (1974)

PROFFER, Carl. The Widows of Russia and Other
   Writings (1987)

PROFFER, Carl, ed. Modern Russian Poets on Poetry: An
   Anthology (1974)

PROFFER, Carl, ed. Russian Romantic Prose: An
   Anthology (1979)

PROFFER, Carl, ed. Soviet Criticism of American
   Literature (1972)

PROFFER, Carl, and MEYER, Ronald. Nineteenth-
   Century Russian Literature in English: A Bibliography
   of Criticism and Translation (1990)

PROFFER, Carl, and MOODY, Fred. Index to "Russian
   Literature Triquarterly," 1971–76 (1978)

PROFFER, Carl, and PROFFER, Ellendea, eds. The Ardis Anthology of Recent Russian Literature (1975)

PROFFER, Carl, and PROFFER, Ellendea, eds. The Ardis Anthology of Russian Futurism (1979)

PROFFER, Carl, and PROFFER, Ellendea, eds. The Barsukov Triangle, The Two-Toned Blonde, and Other Stories (1984)

PROFFER, Carl, and PROFFER, Ellendea, eds. Contemporary Russian Prose (1982)

PROFFER, Carl, and PROFFER, Ellendea, eds. The Silver Age of Russian Culture: An Anthology (1975)

PROFFER, Carl, et al., eds. The Twenties: An Anthology (1987)

PROFFER, Ellendea. Bulgakov: Life and Work (1984)

PROFFER, Ellendea. E. Evreinov: A Pictorial Biography (bilingual) (1981)

PROFFER, Ellendea. International Bibliography of Bulgakov (1976)

PROFFER, Ellendea. Marina Tsvetaeva: A Pictorial Biography/Fotobiografiia (bilingual) (1980)

PROFFER, Ellendea. A Pictorial Biography of M. Bulgakov/Fotobiografiia (bilingual) (1984)

PROFFER, Ellendea. Vladimir Nabokov: A Pictorial Biography (1991)

PRZYBYLSKI, Ryszard. An Essay on the Poetry of Osip Mandelstam (1987)

PURISHKEVICH, V. M. The Murder of Rasputin (1985)

PUSHKIN, Alexander. The Bakhchesarian Fountain and Other Poems by Various Authors (reprint) (1987)

PUSHKIN, Alexander. Collected Narrative and Lyrical Poetry (1984)

PUSHKIN, Alexander. Epigrams and Satirical Verse (1984)

PUSHKIN, Alexander. Eugene Onegin (first Ardis ed., 1993)

PUSHKIN, Alexander. The History of Pugachev (1983)

PUSHKIN, Alexander. A Journey to Arzrum (1974)

PUSHKIN, Alexander. Ruslan and Liudmila (1974)

PUSHKIN, Alexander. Three Comic Poems (1977)

RABINOWITZ, Stanley. The Noise of Change (1986)

RADNOTI, Miklos. The Complete Poetry (1979)

RADNOTI, Miklos. Subway Stops: Fifty Poems (1977)

RAZGON, Lev. True Stories: The Memoirs of Lev Razgon (1996)

RANCOUR-LAFERRIERE, Daniel. The Mind of Stalin (1988)

RANCOUR-LAFERRIERE, Daniel. Out from under Gogol's Overcoat (1982)

REMIZOV, Alexei. Selected Prose (1985)

RICE, James. Dostoevsky and the Healing Art (1985)

RICE, Martin. Valery Briusov and the Rise of Russian Symbolism (1975)

RICHARDSON, William. "Zolotoe Runo" and Russian Modernism (1986)

RIGSBEE, David. Stamping Ground (1976)

RIGSBEE, David, and PROFFER, Ellendea, eds. The Ardis Anthology of New American Poetry (1977)

ROSENBERG, William G. Bolshevik Visions (1984)

ROWE, William Woodin. Holiday Poems (1983)

ROWE, William Woodin. Nabokov and Others: Patterns in Russian Literature (1979)

ROWE, William Woodin. Nabokov's Spectral Dimension (1981)

ROWE, William Woodin. Patterns in Russian Literature II: Notes on Classics (1988)

RUDNITSKY, Konstantin. Meyerhold the Director (1981)

RUSSIAN LITERATURE TRIQUARTERLY (RLT), 24 vols. (1971–1991)

RYDEL, Christine, ed. The Ardis Anthology of Russian Romanticism (1984)

SADOVNIKOV, Dmitry. Riddles of the Russian People (1986)

SALTYKOV-SHCHEDRIN, Mikhail. The Golovlyov Family (1977)

SALTYKOV-SHCHEDRIN, Mikhail. History of a Town (1982)

SALTYKOV-SHCHEDRIN, Mikhail. The Pompadours (1985)

SCHEER, Linda, and FLORES RAMIREZ, Miguel, eds. Poetry of Transition: Mexican Poetry of the 1960s and 1970s (1984)

SCHULTZE, Sydney. The Structure of *Anna Karenina* (1979)

SCOTT, W. B. Chicago Letter and Other Parodies (1976)

SEATON, Jerome. The Wine of Endless Life: Taoist Drinking Songs from the Yuan Dynasty (1978)

SHAGINIAN, Marietta. Mess-Mend: Yankees in Petrograd (1991)

SHELDON, Richard. Viktor Shklovsky: An International Bibliography of Works by and about Him (1977)

SHKLOVSKY, Viktor. Third Factory (1977)

SHUKSHIN, Vasily. "Snowball Berry Red" and Other Stories (1979)

SOKOLOV, Sasha. A School for Fools (1977)

SOLLOGUB, Vladimir. The Tarantas: Impressions of a Journey (1989)

SOLOGUB, Fyodor. Bad Dreams (1978)

TURGENEV, Ivan. Letters, 2 vols. (1983)

TYNIANOV, Yury. The Problem of Verse Language (1979)

VAKHTIN, Boris. The Sheepskin Coat and An Absolutely Happy Village (1988)

VALKENIER, Elizabeth. Russian Realist Art: The State and Society (1977)

VARLAMOVA, Inna. A Counterfeit Life (1988)

VINOGRADOV, V. V. Gogol and the Natural School (1987)

VISSON, Lynn. The Complete Russian Cookbook (1982)

VISSON, Lynn. From Russian into English: An Introduction to Simultaneous Interpretation (bilingual) (1991)

VOGEL, Lucy, ed. Alexander Blok: An Anthology of Critical Essays and Memoirs (1982)

WALTON, David. Waiting in Line (1975)

WAT, Alexander. Mediterranean Poems (1977)

WIEDER, Laurence. No Harm Done (1975)

WILLIAMS, Richard. Savarin (1977)

WYSPIANSKI, Stanislaw. The Wedding (1990)

ZAMIATIN, Evgeny. The Islanders (1978)

ZAMIATIN, Evgeny. A Godforsaken Hole (1988)

ZOSHCHENKO, Mikhail. Before Sunrise (1974)

ZOSHCHENKO, Mikhail. A Man Is Not a Flea (1989)

ZOSHCHENKO, Mikhail. Youth Restored (1985)

Русские издания/Russian Publications

АВВАКУМ, П. Житие протопопа Аввакума (1982)

АКСЕНОВ, В. Бумажный пейзаж (1983)

АКСЕНОВ, В. Золотая наша железка (1980)

БЕРМАН, Ф. Регистратор (1984)

БИРГЕР, Б. Каталог (1975)

БИТОВ, А. Пушкинский дом (1978)

БЛОК, А. Двенадцать (1972)

БРОДСКИЙ, И. Конец прекрасной эпохи (1977)

БРОДСКИЙ, И. Мрамор (1984)

БРОДСКИЙ, И. Новые стансы к Августе (1983)

БРОДСКИЙ, И. Остановка в пустыне (1988)

БРОДСКИЙ, И. Пейзаж с наводнением (1996)

БРОДСКИЙ, И. Урания (1987)

БРОДСКИЙ, И. Часть речи (1977)

БУЛГАКОВ, М. Дьяволиада (1976)

БУЛГАКОВ, М. Зойкина квартира (1971)

БУЛГАКОВ, М. Неизданный Булгаков (1977)

БУЛГАКОВ, М. Собрание сочинений.

Том I: Ранняя проза (1982)

Том II: Ранняя проза (1985)

Том III: Повести (1983)

Том IV: Белая гвардия (1989)

Том VIII: Мастер и Маргарита (1988)

БУЛГАКОВ, М. Фотобиография (1984)

ВАГИНОВ, К. Гарпагониада (1983)

ВАГИНОВ, К. Константин Вагинов (1978)

ВАГИНОВ, К. Путешествие в хаос (1972)

ВАЙЛЬ, П., и ГЕНИС, А. 60-е. Мир советского человека (1988)

ВАРЛАМОВА, И. Мнимая жизнь (1978)

ВАХТИН, Б. Две повести (1982)

ВВЕДЕНСКИЙ, А. Полное собрание сочинений. Том I (1980), Том II (1980)

ВЕРЕСАЕВ, В. В. Гоголь в жизни (1983)

ВЕРЕСАЕВ, В. В. Как работал Гоголь (1983)

ВИНОГРАДОВ, В. В. Стиль прозы Лермонтова (1985)

ВОЙНОВИЧ, В. Антисоветский Советский Союз (1985)

ВОЙНОВИЧ, В. Жизнь и необычайные приключения солдата Ивана Чонкина. Том I (1985), Том II (1985)

ВОЙНОВИЧ, В. Иванькиада (1976)

ВОЙНОВИЧ, В. Москва 2042 (1987)

ВОРОНСКИЙ, А. Статьи (1980)

ГАЗДАНОВ, Г. Вечер у Клэр (1979)

ГЕРШЕНЗОН, М. О. Мудрость Пушкина (1983)

ГИППИУС, З. Письма к Берберовой и Ходасевичу (1978)

ГЛАГОЛ. Литературный альманах. Том I (1977), Том II (1978), Том III (1981)

ГЛАДИЛИН, А. Большой беговой день (1983)

ГЛАДИЛИН, А. Каким я был тогда (1986)

ГОРБАНЕВСКАЯ, Н. Деревянный ангел (1983)

ГОРБАНЕВСКАЯ, Н. Побережье (1973)

ГУМИЛЕВ, Н. К синей звезде (1986)

ГУМИЛЕВ, Н. Костер (1979)

ГУМИЛЕВ, Н. Огненный столп (1975)

ДОВЛАТОВ, С. Наши (1983)

ДОВЛАТОВ, С. Невидимая книга (1978)

ДОВЛАТОВ, С. Ремесло (1985)

ДОСТОЕВСКИЙ, Ф. М. Записки из подполья (1982)

ДУРЫЛИН, С. «Герой нашего времени» М. Ю. Лермонтова (1984)

ЕВРЕИНОВ, Н. Самое главное (1980)

ЕВРЕИНОВ, Н. Фотобиография (1981)

ЕРМАКОВ, И. Д. Этюды по психологии творчества А.С. Пушкина (1980)

ЕСЕНИН, С. Избранные стихи (1979)

ЕФИМОВ, И. Как одна плоть (1981)

ЕФИМОВ, И. Практическая метафизика (1980)

ЖАР-ПТИЦА No. 1 (1983) журнал

ЗАБОЛОЦКИЙ, Н. Столбцы (1975)

ЗАМЯТИН, Е. Наводнение (1976)

ЗАМЯТИН, Е. Нечестивые рассказы (1978)

ЗАМЯТИН, Е. Островитяне (1979)

ЗЕРКАЛОВ, А. Евангелие Михаила Булгакова (1983)

ЗОЩЕНКО, М. Неизданный Зощенко (1977)

ЗОЩЕНКО, М. Рассказы (1979)

ЗОЩЕНКО, М., и ПИЛЬНЯК, Б. Статьи и материалы (1971)

ЗУНДЕЛОВИЧ, Я. Романы Достоевского (1984)

ИВАНОВ, В., и ГЕРШЕНЗОН, М. О. Переписка из двух углов (1980)

ИСКАНДЕР, Ф. Кролики и удавы (1982)

ИСКАНДЕР, Ф. Новые главы. Сандро из Чегема (1981)

ИСКАНДЕР, Ф. Сандро из Чегема (1979)

КАЙЗЕР, Р. Россия: Власть и народ (1979)

КАТАЛОГ: Литературный альманах (1982)

КЕНЖЕЕВ, Б. Избранная лирика. 1970–1981 (1984)

КИРЕЕВСКИЙ, И. Полное собрание сочинений. В двух томах (1983)

КОПЕЛЕВ, Л. Вера в слово (1977)

КОПЕЛЕВ, Л. Держава и народ (1982)

КОПЕЛЕВ, Л. И сотворил себе кумира (1978)

КОПЕЛЕВ, Л. Утоли моя печали (1981)

КОПЕЛЕВ, Л. Хранить вечно (1975)

КОЭН, С. Бухарин [with Strathcona Press] (1980)

КРЕПС, М. О поэзии Иосифа Бродского (1984)

КУБЛАНОВСКИЙ, Ю. Избранное (1981)

КУЗМИН, М. Вожатый (1979)

КУЗМИН, М. Занавешанные картинки (1972)

КУЗМИН, М. Крылья (1979)

КУЗМИН, М. Форель разбивает лед (1978)

ЛИМОНОВ, Э. Русское (1979)

ЛИПКИН, С. Воля (1981)

ЛИПКИН, С. Кочевой огонь (1984)

ЛИПКИН, С. Сталинград Василия Гроссмана (1986)

ЛИСНЯНСКАЯ, И. Стихотворения (1984)

МАКСУДОВ, С. (сост.) Неуслышанные голоса.
    Документы Смоленского архива (1987)

МАНДЕЛЬШТАМ, О. Воронежские тетради (1980)

МАНДЕЛЬШТАМ, О. Египетская марка (1977)

МАНДЕЛЬШТАМ, О. Камень (1971)

МАНДЕЛЬШТАМ, О. Проза (1983)

МАНДЕЛЬШТАМ, О. Разговор о Данте (1983)

МАНДЕЛЬШТАМ, О. Tristia (1972)

МАРАМЗИН, В. Блондин обеего цвета (1975)

МАРАМЗИН, В. Тянитолкай (1981)

МАЯКОВСКИЙ, В. Владимир Маяковский —
    Трагедия (1977)

МАЯКОВСКИЙ, В. Про это (1973)

МЕТРОПОЛЬ. Литературный альманах (1979)

МИЛОСЛАВСКИЙ, Ю. От шума всадников и
    стрелков (1984)

МИЛОШ, Ч. Поэтический трактат (1982)

МИНЧИН, А. Псих (1995)

МИХАЙЛОВ, М. Планетарное сознание (1982)

НАБОКОВ, В. Аня в стране чудес (1982)

НАБОКОВ, В. Бледный огонь (1983)

НАБОКОВ, В. Весна в Фиальте (1978)

НАБОКОВ, В. Возвращение Чорба (1976)

НАБОКОВ, В. Дар (1975)

НАБОКОВ, В. Другие берега (1978)

НАБОКОВ, В. Защита Лужина (1979)

НАБОКОВ, В. Камера обскура (1978)

НАБОКОВ, В. Король, дама, валет (1979)

НАБОКОВ, В. Лолита (1976)

НАБОКОВ, В. Машенька (1974)

НАБОКОВ, В. Отчаяние (1978)

НАБОКОВ, В. Переписка с сестрой (1985)

НАБОКОВ, В. Пнин (1983)

НАБОКОВ, В. Подвиг (1974)

НАБОКОВ, В. Приглашение на казнь (1979)

НАБОКОВ, В. Собрание сочинений.

    Том I: Король, дама, валет. Машенька (1987)

    Том III: Соглядатай. Волшебник (1991)

    Том VI: Дар (1989)

    Том X: Лолита (1989)

НАБОКОВ, В. Соглядатай (1978)

НАБОКОВ, В. Стихи (1979)

НАППЕЛЬБАУМ, М. Наш век (1983)

ОКУДЖАВА, Б. 65 песен. Том I (1980), Том II (1986)

ОЛЕША, Ю. Зависть (1977)

ОРЛОВА, Р. Воспоминание о непрошедшем времени (1983)

ОРЛОВА, Р. Хемингуэй в России (1985)

ОРЛОВА, Р., и Копелев, Л. Мы жили в Москве (1988)

ПАПЕРНЫЙ, В. Культура «два». Советская архитектура 1932–1954 (1985)

ПАРНОК, С. Собрание стихотворений (1979)

ПАСТЕРНАК, Б. Воздушные пути (1976)

ПАСТЕРНАК, Б. Сестра моя жизнь (1976)

ПАСТЕРНАК, Б. Темы и вариации (1972)

ПАТЕРА, Т. Обзор творчества Юрия Трифонова (1983)

ПИЛЬНЯК, Б. Голый год (1979)

ПИЛЬНЯК, Б. Красное дерево (1979)

ПЛАТОНОВ, А. Котлован (1973)

ПЛАТОНОВ, А. Шарманка (1975)

ПОЛЯКОВА, С. Осип Мандельштам (1989)

ПОЛЯКОВА, С. Закатные оны дни. Цветаева и
    Парнок (1983)

ПОПОВ, Е. Веселие Руси (1981)

ПОРТФЕЛЬ. Литературный альманах (1996)

ПУШКИН, А. Путешествие в Арзрум (1978)

СКОБОЛЕВ, В. (сост.) Творчество Платонова. Статьи
    и сообщения (1986)

СМИТ, М. Парк имени Горького (1985)

СОБОЛЬ, А. Любовь на Арбате (1979)

СОВРЕМЕННЫЕ ЗАПИСКИ. No. 70, 1940 (1983)

СОКОЛОВ, С. Между собакой и волком (1980)

СОКОЛОВ, С. Палисандрия (1985)

СОКОЛОВ, С. Школа для дураков (1976)

СОЛОГУБ, Ф. Мелкий бес (1979)

СОСНОРА, В. Избранное (1987)

СТРЕЛЕЦ, No. 1 (1978)

СУСЛОВ, А. Шесть сонмов. Плакун-город (1986)

ТОМАШЕВСКИЙ, Б. Теория литературы (1972)

ТРИФОНОВ, Ю. Дом на набережной (1983)

ТЫНЯНОВ, Ю. Архаисты и новаторы (1985)

УФЛЯНД, В. Тексты 1955–77 (1978)

ХАКСЛИ, О. Кром желтый (1983)

ХЛЕБНИКОВ, В. Зангези (1984)

ХОДАСЕВИЧ, В. Из еврейских поэтов (1983)

ХОДАСЕВИЧ, В. Письма В. Ф. Ходасевича к Борису
    Садовскому (1983)

INDEX

CPSIA information can be obtained
at www.ICGtesting.com
Printed in the USA
BVOW07*1024220417
480943BV00010B/1/P